Angus Whitson studied law at Edinburgh University and has worked as a solicitor, independent financial adviser and freelance copywriter. He writes the weekly column in the *Dundee Courier*, 'Man With Two Dogs', with two books published on this theme.

Andrew Orr served as a doctor in the Scots Guards and was later a GP in Montrose for many years. He is a founder member of the Montrose Heritage Trust and chairman of the Montrose Bamse Project.

Sea Dog Bamse

World War II Canine Hero

Angus Whitson and Andrew Orr

To Thalia

As a memory of

the visit to Norway

August 2014

Else and
Sverre
Tannum

BIRLINN

This edition first published in 2009 by
Birlinn Limited
West Newington House
10 Newington Road
Edinburgh
EH9 1QS

www.birlinn.co.uk

2

ISBN: 978 1 84158 849 0

British Library Cataloguing-in-Publication Data
A catalogue record for this book is available
from the British Library

Typeset by Brinnoven, Livingston
Printed and bound by CPI Group (UK) Ltd, Croydon, CR0 4YY

To Henny King,
without whose vision and application a statue would not
have been created, and this story may not have been told

*All knowledge, the totality of all questions
and answers, is contained in the dog.*

Franz Kafka

Contents

A Message from Jilly Cooper

When I wrote my book, *Animals in War*, Bamse, the glorious Norwegian St Bernard dog, was easily one of the most charming, courageous, enterprising and charismatic characters in the story of World War II.

I am enchanted that he is honoured by his own wonderful biography. Andrew Orr and Angus Whitson have unearthed a wealth of new material, including fascinating interviews with people who really knew Bamse. I am sure that if you hear a rumble of thunder and see the clouds move on the day this book is published it will be Bamse barking with joy and wagging his tail in heaven.

Jilly Cooper

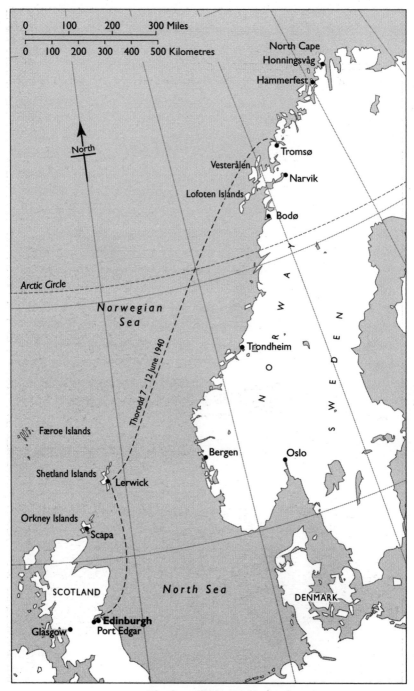

0   100   200   300 Miles

0 100 200 300 400 500 Kilometres

North

North Cape
Honningsvåg
Hammerfest

Tromsø
Vesterålen
Narvik
Lofoten Islands
Bodø

Arctic Circle

Norwegian
Sea

N O R W A Y

S W E D E N

Thorodd 7 - 12 June 1940

Trondheim

Færoe Islands

Shetland Islands
Lerwick

Bergen

Oslo

Orkney Islands
Scapa

SCOTLAND

North Sea

DENMARK

Glasgow

Edinburgh
Port Edgar

Northern Waters 1939–45

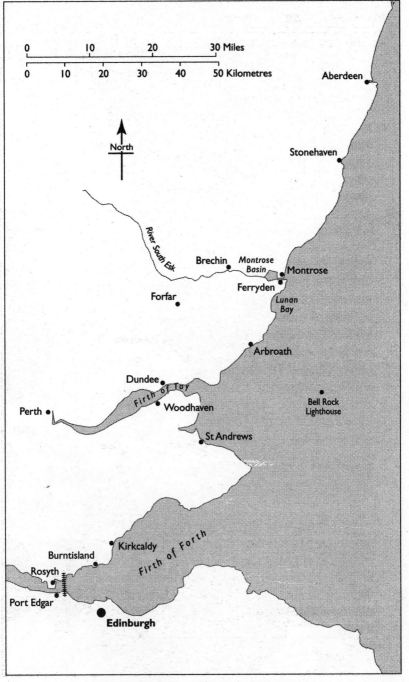

East Scotland Mine Clearance Sector 1941–5

Dundee Docks Area 1939–45

Map labels:

BROUGHTY FERRY ROAD
Shipyard
Fish Dock
• Place where drowning sailor saved
To Arbroath
ARBROATH ROAD
FORFAR ROAD
To Forfar
BROUGHTY FERRY ROAD
Munitions Factory
Eastern Wharves
KNM Nordhav
KNM Thorodd
KNM Borthind
KNM Syrian
(71st Minesweeper Group)
North Sea
King George Wharf
EAST DOCK STREET
CAMPERDOWN STREET
Camperdown Dock
Camperdown West Wharf
River Tay
Victoria Dock
Place where knife attack happened
Customs House
Dock
Empress Ballroom
SEAGATE
MURRAYGATE
Bodega Bar
Albert Institute
HIGH STREET
City Square
CITY CENTRE
HMS Unicorn (Area Naval HQ)
Tidal Dock
Earl Grey Dock
Ferry Dock
Ferry to Newport on Tay
NETHERGATE
Royal Hotel
Station
Queen's Hotel
S. TAY STREET
LOCHEE ROAD
Dundee Royal Infirmary
North
Locarno Ballroom
PERTH ROAD
To Perth
Caird Rest
(Norwegian Mess/Club)

0   1/4   1/2   1 kilometre
0   1/4 miles

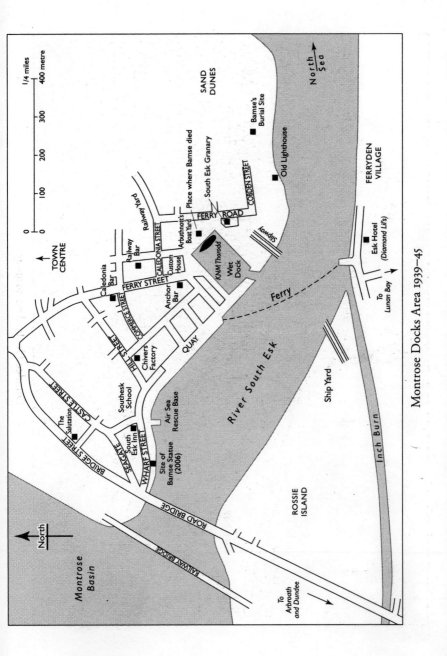

Montrose Docks Area 1939–45

Introduction

Sea dogs and their stories abound throughout naval and maritime history. A wolfhound accompanied Christopher Columbus on his fourth voyage of discovery across the Atlantic Ocean and helped repulse an attack on the garrison Columbus established at Panama. The splendidly named 18th-century admiral Sir Cloudesley Shovell, scarcely remembered now but regarded as the finest admiral of Queen Anne's navy, had his favourite Italian greyhound on board with him when his flagship, *Association*, foundered on the Scilly Isles during a disastrous storm. Perhaps the greyhound had drowned by the time dog and master were cast up together on the island's rocks, but in any event it proved no help to Sir Cloudesley – his throat was cut by an island woman who then stole his emerald rings. Peggy was a bulldog who served with Admiral Sir John Jellicoe on HMS *Iron Duke* at the Battle of Jutland on 31 May 1916. She helped maintain the crew's morale throughout the noise and tumult of the most important sea battle of World War I.

In more recent military history, the events of World War II are peppered with tales of dogs and other animals that behaved with great heroism and inspired the men of the units to which they were attached. This story is about perhaps the most remarkable of all these wartime animals, a fighting sea dog and a ship's mascot who not only served and inspired his fellow crew members, but was renowned across Europe and beyond as a patriotic symbol of loyalty and freedom.

Bamse (pronounced 'Bum-sa'), known as 'the largest dog of all the Allied Forces' was a friendly giant, over six feet tall when he stood upright on his hind legs, and with a hefty build and muscles indicative of his 100-kilogram frame. Wearing his sailor's cap emblazoned with its Kongelige Norske Marine (KNM = Royal Norwegian Navy) ribbon, he was instantly recognisable as the gentle Viking who had, with his king, escaped by sea from German-occupied Norway in 1940, and was engaged in fighting for the liberation of his country.

Bamse was originally bought as a puppy for his master's four children. He was the gentlest of animals with his human companions; indeed, his name in Norwegian means 'teddy bear' or simply 'teddy' – an apt name for the St Bernard who began his life as a much-loved family pet, though it concealed the depth of character and courage of the animal who was to become a dog of war. But for the outbreak of World War II in 1939, Bamse might have grown up in a secure, happy family environment, knowing little more excitement than chasing balls and sticks and giving piggy-back rides to his child companions. As it was, he took his place in the roll-call of conspicuously brave animals who repaid their human masters' trust with selfless loyalty.

Bamse went to war with his master Erling Hafto, who commanded the Royal Norwegian Navy ship KNM *Thorodd* (pronounced 'Too-rod'). During minesweeping patrols protecting the Atlantic and North Sea convoys in World War II, Bamse saw action, taking his place on *Thorodd*'s bow gun platform with his own made-to-measure steel helmet to protect him from enemy fire. His composure in action and his contribution to the ship's morale had a tangible effect on *Thorodd*'s crew, who regarded him as their good-luck symbol and adopted him as ship's mascot. He displayed a true fighting disposition on a number of occasions when he defied attacking German fighter planes and was challenged by other dogs and, remarkably, when he saved a fellow Free Norwegian Navy officer from a knife-wielding assailant.

Word spread of the dog's devotion to duty and his self-control and indifference under fire. Soon he was adopted as mascot of the entire Royal Norwegian Navy, and then of all the Free Norwegian Forces. Reports of Bamse's legendary wartime exploits were told and retold, and the dog's great contribution to morale in the dark days of war eventually inspired much of the Allied Forces fighting in Europe and beyond.

Thorodd operated mainly from the Scottish east-coast ports of Montrose and Dundee, and Bamse became as familiar a figure to residents of the area as to his shipboard companions. His death in July 1944 on the quayside at Montrose, just yards from his beloved *Thorodd*, was somewhat undistinguished compared with his wartime exploits. However, the effect on *Thorodd*'s crew and the loss to the community was profound, such was the universal respect for the dignified dog. Today, Bamse is still regarded as a national hero in his native Norway and his memory has been rekindled in Scotland with the unveiling by HRH Prince Andrew, himself a Royal Navy captain, of a larger-than-life statue of Bamse on Montrose harbour front.

Erling Hafto's daughter Vigdis, who was only a child when Bamse sailed to fight his war, attended the unveiling ceremony, as did a number of Norwegian veterans. Montrosians, especially those who remembered the legendary dog, turned out in crowds for the event to honour his memory. A special message from His Majesty King Harald V of Norway was read by the Royal Norwegian Consul, all confirming the special bond of friendship between the Scottish and Norwegian peoples forged during the uncertainties of war and sustained, in no small part, by the shared affection for this canine symbol of freedom.

Bamse was an exceptional dog who lived an extraordinary life. What follows is the account of the most unconventional ship's mascot in naval annals; an animal who not only found a place in the hearts of his sailor comrades, but also left enduring memories with the civilian population of Scotland, especially in his adopted hometown of Montrose.

1

Norway's Nose

The clatter of a handcart's iron-rimmed wheels on the uneven surface of the cobbled streets drew sympathetic glances from passers-by in the far-northern fishing town. On the handcart lay a little girl, just two years old and desperately ill. She was being taken home from the doctor's tiny infirmary to die. There was nothing more that Dr Harald Borgeresen could do, and he had broken the news to the frightened parents as gently as possible. The child's pinched, white face peeped out from blankets piled deep to cushion her from the jolts and bumps of the rough journey. Despite the near sub-zero temperature, her small hand stretched out from beneath the blankets, clutching the hand of her mother, who walked alongside.

It was a short journey from the infirmary to the family home, up the hill past traditional three-storey wooden houses painted dark blue, magenta and cream. In the tight-knit fishing community everyone knew each other; happy events were celebrated and misfortunes were shared by all. Everyone was touched by the little girl's sickness, from which there seemed small hope of recovery. No one passed the cart without words of encouragement and support, and some came out of their houses to ask after her. The father strained at the cart's shafts, struggling to ease the rigid wheels over the worst of the ruts. A warm bed heated with earthenware hot-water bottles had been prepared for the small patient, and the mother urged her husband to hurry home out of the bitter weather. The father, no less concerned for their beloved daughter, did his best to calm his distraught wife, pointing out that to go any faster could worsen little Vigdis' condition. At home, the patient's older sisters and brother waited apprehensively for their parents' return, watched over by Bamse, the family's two-year-old St Bernard dog, who was already showing the reliability and the steadiness of temperament which were to characterise the rest of his life.

Near the top of the hill, where the houses thinned and familiar views over the harbour and the fjord opened out, the makeshift conveyance reached the patient's home. Bamse's broad face, staring intently from a front window, disappeared abruptly, and the dog joined the family's older children as they flung open the front door and trooped out quietly to welcome their little sister home. Bamse seemed to sense the sadness and gravity of the situation, and his normal ecstatic greeting, capering and frisking round the family was subdued. The tawny head pushed over the blankets, and after a couple of confirmatory sniffs his pink tongue licked the little girl's hand. It was no burden for the father to carry his daughter's feather-light body to the warm bed, where her mother undressed her. Her siblings went with their father to the kitchen, where he explained the doctor's prognosis and prepared them for Vigdis' almost certain death.

In this most northern part of Norway, with its sense of being at the extreme end of the known world, everyone was familiar with death – it is said that at one time every fourth adult male died at sea. These were the days before the wonders of available antibiotics – unlike today, when doctors have a pharmacopoeia of proprietary drugs and remedies with which to attack every illness and ailment. Before World War II, epidemic illnesses were expected and commonplace, not just in Norway, but worldwide. Childhood epidemics, especially, were frequently fatal as doctors had so few means of combating them. The fisher folk of the village were no strangers to adversity, and such deaths were accepted with fortitude and stoicism.

No one had time to give much thought to the dog, who had come into the bedroom with the family and lain down beside the bed. When the girl's mother had done all she could to ensure her daughter's comfort, she called Bamse to follow her through to the kitchen and join the rest of the family. But the dog remained where he was, and nothing anyone – not even his master – said or did could persuade him to leave the patient's side.

From that moment Bamse took charge. Only the mother and the doctor could enter the little girl's bedroom. As if by some incredible instinct, he seemed to understand that these were the two people best able to care for his smallest charge. All others, including her father, the dog physically debarred from entering. Thus began Bamse's remarkable vigil, and he did not move from the bedside except to feed and attend the calls of nature. At such times her father and siblings surely snatched a few moments to visit the patient, but made sure they were out of the bedroom by the time the great nanny dog returned.

For 12 days and nights the dog kept his watch. There is only hearsay about the patient's progress, because the sole person still alive to tell the story is Vigdis herself. As she was so young, she has no memory of coming so close to death, and indeed has never known what she was suffering from. At that age, children sleep much of the day, and the recuperative power of sleep is well acknowledged. To the wonder of the waiting and watching family, the frail child passed through a period of crisis and then gradually began to show signs of recovery, sleeping round the clock and waking only to be fed and changed by her mother.

The prayers of the family had been answered. News of Vigdis' merciful recovery rapidly spread to neighbours and soon to the rest of the community. The dog's 12-day vigil, which had begun so hopelessly, ended joyfully with the complete recovery of the little girl who had been sent home to die. Everyone marvelled at Bamse's intervention, and there was much debate about his contribution to Vigdis' restoration to full health. Most agreed that it was nothing short of a miracle, and it was an early indication of the dog's insight and comprehension of human conditions, that developed in such an astounding way in later years.

It seems probable that it was at this point that Bamse began to establish his reputation as a dog far beyond the ordinary. It says something about Bamse that he had the innate confidence to impose his will on his master, and it says something about the father, Erling Hafto, a former naval officer, and presumably not greatly used to being opposed, that he accepted the domestic regime imposed by the family pet. However, something profound must have connected between the two, because in due course they sailed off together to fight a war.

The little girl, Vigdis Hafto, at the time of writing in 2008, is a grandmother in her seventies and a picture of good health. She shows no sign of how close to death she was all those years ago.

If the incidental details of this story have been embellished, in general the events happened as they are told. It all took place

in 1938 in Honningsvåg, a fishing and whaling centre and the
principal town on the south coast of the island of Magerøya at
the extreme north of Norway. It was here that Vigdis grew up
with Bamse as her constant companion. Captain Hafto was
Honningsvåg's harbour-master, a job central to the life of the
community, and consequently he was one of the town's leading
men. The title 'captain' was not a reference to naval rank, but
one accorded him as a courtesy in his capacity as harbour-master.
It seems strange now that a man of his authority and standing
should have had only an ordinary handcart to transport his
dying daughter home, but in 1938 Honningsvåg was about as
remote a spot in Europe as it was possible to be.

Magerøya Island lies 525 kilometres north of the Arctic Circle –
at a similar latitude to Point Barrow in the very north of Alaska –
at the very northernmost tip of Europe. There is no landmass
between it and the North Pole over 2,000 kilometres away.
Almost everything about Magerøya and Honningsvåg – the
church, the school, the harbour – always has been, and still is,
'the world's most northernmost'. Russian sailors, on their way
from the Atlantic Ocean to the Russian port of Murmansk
on the Barents Sea, sailed past the steep cliffs of Nordkapp
(North Cape) on Magerøya's north coast, and nicknamed it
'Norway's Nose'. In 1938 the only link with the mainland was
by boat across the one-kilometre-wide Magerøya Sound, and
fishing and agriculture were practically the only commercial
activities on the island. Roads were cobbled, and only tracks
linked the main town with the outlying villages. Apart from a
few commercial vehicles at the harbour, there were no cars. The
old town had grown up long before the invention of the internal
combustion engine, and its narrow streets were not suited to
motor traffic; in any case, Honningsvåg's whole *raison d'être* at

that time was fishing and whaling, so boats were the principal means of transportation. Erling Hafto, therefore, could not call for an ambulance to speed his daughter's journey home from hospital.

Today the island is linked to the mainland by the sub-sea Nordkapp (North Cape) Tunnel. While fishing still forms a core business activity, the island has become increasingly dependent on tourism, and the port of Honningsvåg is a popular cruise-ship destination. It is a land of contrasts: in summer the constant daylight from the never-setting sun brings a surge of energy and activity, while from November until January the sun sinks below the horizon, with the semi-darkness lightened by dazzling displays of the dancing Aurora Borealis, the breathtaking Northern Lights. Mythical bedtime stories of supernatural trolls who steal naughty children's minds and enslave them contrast with the hard reality of daily life within the Arctic Circle.

Honningsvåg is situated at the foot of the east arc of a horseshoe-shaped fjord at the south end of the island, overlooking Magerøya Sound and the steep cliff faces and dramatic mountains of the mainland beyond. To the south lies the mouth and dark waters of the Porsangen fjord, an inlet of the Barents Sea. The harbour provides a deepwater anchorage, safe in almost all weathers, which explains why the whale catchers and fishermen built their community in such a lonely spot. It would be natural to think that so close to the Arctic ice cap Norway's northern coast would be ice-bound, at least for some months of the year; but it is not so.

The Gulf Stream system of warm ocean currents keeps the coasts of this part of northern Europe free of ice all year round. The currents originate off the tip of Florida and travel north up America's eastern seaboard and across the North Atlantic to become the North Atlantic Drift, which splits. One branch heads south past the Canary Islands, skirting the coasts of southwest Europe and western Africa. The other continues northwards, warming Scotland's west coast on its way, to feed the Norwegian Current. It swirls past Norway's Nose as it journeys east along Russia's north coast and peters out, eventually, somewhere in the Barents Sea. All along the northeast aspect of Norway's fjord-pitted coastline, and then eastwards past the Russian port of Murmansk, the warm currents keep the Arctic ice at bay and the seaways open.

Thanks to the Gulf Stream, in winter the temperature at Honningsvåg is some 20°C higher than other areas at this latitude. The warm currents carry nutrients that fish feed on, which in turn attract the sea birds that follow the fish. It is small wonder that for generations fishing has been a way of life and culture for these northern people. Cod, haddock, pollack, salmon, halibut and shellfish support a large fishing industry, and the waters abound with seals, dolphins, and killer and minke whales, which traditionally provided food and a source of profit for their hunters.

The combination of an open seaway, a sheltered deepwater harbour and an abundance of sea harvest allowed about 4,000 people to subsist on Magerøya, with just over half of them living in Honningsvåg. The number seems to defy the landscape they clung to – wind-torn, rocky, treeless and barren. Not surprisingly, they were outnumbered by the reindeer, which are far more suited to such a remote place.

It was in this stark landscape that Bamse's story unfolded. With the mountain ancestry of the St Bernard, a breed that originated in the Himalayas and evolved in the Italian Alps, Bamse was well suited to these Arctic conditions and his subsequent life at sea. He may have seemed just a great bundle of cosy fur, but he represented his breed well as a muscular, northern-climate working dog, and he would not have felt out of his element in the remote region to which his master Erling Hafto brought him.

2

Family Matters

Erling Hafto was born in 1900 in Nedre Eiker, near Oslo, into an entirely different world from the one where he was to spend most of his life, 1,600 kilometres north in Honningsvåg. Not only are there geographical differences, but there is also a distinctness of culture and language. Northern Scandinavia, where Honningsvåg lies, is the home of the indigenous Sami people, who inhabit a vast expanse of territory lying across four nations. The area includes Finnmark and North Troms in Norway, the northern counties of Sweden, Lapland in Finland and the adjacent Kola Peninsula in Russia; it is the land of trolls, reindeer and Santa Claus. The Sami homelands are as alien to the people of Oslo as the Outer Hebrides off Scotland's west coast, with their Gaelic-speaking inhabitants, are to residents of London. For Erling Hafto, Honningsvåg was a remote place far from his family and his upbringing. It was the sea that brought him to Honningsvåg, and it was the sea took him away to war, before returning him there for the rest of his working life.

From childhood, Erling wanted only to go to sea, and at fifteen he successfully applied for a naval cadetship aboard a sail training ship, the traditional way of entering the Royal Norwegian Navy. He never regretted this early choice and thrived in his new element. Family papers indicate that he was the top cadet of his intake, showing outstanding leadership qualities. He went on to graduate as an officer from the Royal Norwegian Naval Academy.

Given this promising start, it is surprising that Erling decided to leave the navy in 1925, when he was only 25. There are no obvious reasons for this. He plainly did not want to abandon a seagoing life as he was soon engaged by a shipping company as captain of a coastal vessel, plying trade up and down the length of Norway. Pay and conditions may have been better with his new employers, or his decision to leave the navy may have been influenced by meeting his future wife, Halldis, who came from the coastal town of Bodø, the second-largest town of northern Norway. The couple may have fallen in love when Erling's ship called into the port, which is a centre for shipbuilding and repair. It is notoriously difficult for a sailor to keep romance alive when he is away from shore for extended periods, and Halldis may have made it clear that the life of a sailor's wife was not for her.

Their marriage in 1927 was to last for nearly fifty years. In 1928, their first child, Kjersti, was born in Bodø. She was followed in 1932 by another daughter, Torbjør. For as long as Erling continued to work at sea, he endured the separations of each voyage. His daughter Vigdis remembers how his family meant everything to her father, and how he hated being away from his wife and children. A desire to settle his family in a stable environment led him to seek a position on land that would make use of his marine experience. In such a seafaring environment there was no shortage of sailors like him who were ready to sling their anchor on shore, and competition was strong whenever suitable posts became available, so it is testimony to his abilities that at the age of only 31 he was appointed assistant harbour-

master at Honningsvåg. Erling and his young family then moved
to the port, and it was there that a son, Gunnar-Helge, was born
in 1933. In 1935, their youngest child Vigdis arrived.

In the year of Vigdis' birth, Erling was promoted to harbour-
master of Honningsvåg. This was an important post because
of the volume of fishing boats and commercial ships that used
the port. He was now in a secure government position which
allowed him to settle down, establish a family home and plan
for a future. His office was on the main quay in the centre of the
town's commercial activities, and the house they lived in was at
the top of the hill overlooking the fjord. When not in the office,
Erling was seen riding his horse to and from work and around
the island when he visited the small outlying fishing harbours.
As harbour-master he was central to the commercial life of the
port, but Erling was also an outgoing and friendly man and the
Hafto family soon played a leading role in Honningsvåg's social
life, and an international sprinkling of sea captains from all over
Europe, especially Britain, regularly called at the Hafto house
on the hill. The children learned to speak excellent English,
hearing it spoken from an early age.

After Vigdis' birth, Halldis may have thought that the family
was complete, but Erling produced a surprise. Twice a year he
travelled to Oslo to present his reports to the authorities on the
past half-year's activities at Honningsvåg port. It was a long and
slow journey, and he was usually away from home for several
weeks, but it gave him the opportunity to visit his family at
Nedre Eiker. Like any fond husband and father he returned
home from these trips laden with special gifts for his family
from the distant capital city of Oslo.

On one of his trips in 1937 he visited a dog breeder near his
old family home, and bought a pedigree St Bernard puppy. It

is not known whether he had long planned to own such a large family pet, or whether he was captivated by what he saw and bought the puppy on impulse, but he was certainly the first of many who fell under the spell of this particular dog. Whatever his motivation, the puppy accompanied him home as a pet for his children. What Halldis said when her husband presented her with the newest addition to the family can only be guessed at, but with four active children, the youngest only one year old, she might at the very least have suggested his timing was misplaced. Most likely the whole family was involved in choosing a name for their pet and after much discussion, especially amongst the children, everyone agreed upon Bamse.

St Bernards, or Saints, as they are also affectionately known, are one of the most readily recognisable breeds of dog, and one of the largest. Although they are gentle-natured dogs and make ideal pets, it takes a particular type of person and family to take on responsibility for a Saint, as they must be prepared to make room in their lives and home for a very bulky addition. On his arrival in Honningsvåg, Bamse became the most northerly St Bernard in the world, for there is no suggestion that there were any others of his breed on the island. He settled into his new family and surroundings much like any puppy, although he needed more space than the average family pet. At this time, houses on treeless Magerøya were built almost entirely of wood, every piece of which had to be imported from the extensive forests on the mainland. As a result, wood was not to be used extravagantly in house construction, and although the rooms were adequate in size, they were not spacious. A growing St Bernard dog took up more space and posed a bigger problem than a growing child in the Haftos' relatively small home.

A puppy the size of a Labrador needs feeding on a grand scale, and, as he matured, Bamse's appetite grew with him. Little can be told about his diet, but he seems to have been influenced by his environment because he acquired a taste for raw fish, possibly out of desperation to satisfy his hunger pangs. It was a taste that would stand him in good stead in later years.

The St Bernard breed we know today was established in the Great St Bernard hospice and monastery founded *c.*1050 by an Augustinian monk, Saint Bernard of Menthon, at the wild alpine pass that bears his name. The Great St Bernard Pass marks the border between Switzerland and Italy, and, at 2,469 metres, is the highest point on what was once a busy trading and pilgrimage route between the two countries. There are no accurate records of the breed's true origins and development but it seems generally agreed that St Bernards were descended from Tibetan mastiffs, possibly left behind at the monastery by travellers and kept by the monks, initially, as guard dogs.

Tibetan mastiffs are mountain dogs and their sturdy bone structure and large, broad heads are replicated in the St Bernard. Like their ancestors, Saints have a thick coat to repel the worst weathers and have developed their own colouration, typically red-brown or tawny with white markings. Tibetan mastiffs were originally flock- and guard-dogs, and Bamse was proficient in both roles, learning first to look after and safely shepherd the Hafto children when they visited their father at his office, and later, in Scotland, rounding up *Thorodd*'s crew after nights out drinking and guarding the ship against unwelcome visitors.

The three youngest children became Bamse's special charges and companions, although Vigdis says that while he was the family pet and shared by all, it was generally acknowledged that he showed his greatest allegiance to her. The eldest daughter Kjersti, aged nine when Bamse arrived, was at school and too

independent to admit to needing a four-footed minder. The
four youngest members of the family – including Bamse now –
were thrown together, and as the puppy grew, inevitably faster
than his human companions, the children looked to him for
friendship and comfort. They perhaps even regarded him as
gang leader. From early on, Bamse began to display common
sense, dependability and all of the other positive traits of his
breed, responding well to the trust that the children and their
parents put in him.

It took pressure off Halldis, despite her initial reservations,
to know that the big nanny dog was so protective towards the
children. As the friendship between dog and children developed
and their reliance on him grew his influence spread beyond the
immediate Hafto family. Vigdis remembers when he grew big
enough to give the smaller children rides on his back, and it was
not long before he was a favourite amongst all the neighbouring
families. As his coat thickened, the young children used him as
they might an electric blanket, snuggling up to him for warmth.
Scarcely out of puppyhood, he already displayed a patience with
the demands of children that would normally be exceptional in
an adult dog, and he became the children's constant playmate.

As he grew stronger and his usefulness became apparent, a
harness with two large panniers for carrying food and shopping
was made for him. In the winter, he was harnessed to a sledge
and delighted the children with his willingness to provide sleigh
rides. He accepted all of these tasks with equanimity and clear
enjoyment, as though they were his contribution to his adoptive
family's well-being. As he matured, a pattern of behaviour
emerged which marked him out as a dog with an outstanding
affinity for human beings. The defining incident early on in his
life, which cemented the esteem held for him not only within

the Hafto family, but by all the people of Honningsvåg, was his long vigil over Vigdis and her incredible recovery.

Thereafter, the Hafto parents were confident that they could leave their younger children alone in Bamse's safekeeping and that he would ensure that they came to no harm. The children were regular visitors to their father's office at the harbour and they clung tightly onto Bamse's fur as he guided them safely there and home again. Island life in pre-World War II Norway was pretty safe for young children, slower and more tranquil than on the mainland – closer to nature and lacking many of mainland living amenities. There were no motor vehicles to avoid, but the sea could be dangerous, and although everyone knew everybody else and kept an eye on youngsters wandering where they shouldn't, it was impossible to be alert constantly to what children were up to. Bamse had proved he could anticipate danger and divert the children from it.

Regardless of the affection she and the whole family felt for him, however, Halldis found Bamse's increasingly hefty physical presence very intrusive as he took up more and more space in the family home. Even though he contributed much to the Hafto family life, Halldis found it increasingly difficult to cope with him, especially on her own when her husband was away. St Bernards are generally not fully grown until they are at least two years old, and Bamse grew to be very large, even by the breed standards of the time. Despite the maturity he had displayed while he was growing up, as he approached his second birthday he still behaved like a puppy from time to time, displaying a bouncy, jolly temperament and knocking over children, and even adults, in his enthusiasm for life and people. One sweep of his tail could clear a table of everything upon it. Although her mother may have wished that her husband had not come home with such an unsuitable pet for her small house, Vigdis makes it clear that a deep, durable bond grew up between herself and her nanny dog, and this bond was never severed by distance or by time.

There was to be an unexpected solution to Halldis' problem, which she herself provided. As events turned out, however, Halldis would have gladly settled for the status quo had she known the full extent of the horrors that would follow as Europe slipped towards the unthinkable, a second world war.

3

Rumbles of War

A dolf Hitler was appointed Reich Chancellor of Germany on 30 January 1933. He immediately used his position as leader to consolidate power in the National Socialist German Workers Party, or the Nazi Party, for short. One of his early moves was to order the remilitarisation of Germany, which was in direct violation of the Treaty of Versailles that Germany had signed after its defeat in World War I. Hitler's vision was to reunite all the German-speaking peoples of Europe, and after the military reoccupation of the Rhineland in March 1936 – which again violated the terms of the Treaty of Versailles – he turned his sights on Austria, which was annexed in March 1938.

He was encouraged by the subdued response to these actions, especially from Great Britain and France, and his next move was towards the German Sudetenland of Czechoslovakia. In pursuit of a policy of appeasement, Britain and France signed the Munich Agreement on 29 September 1938, turning over the Sudetenland to Germany in exchange for German promises to pursue no further territorial goals. Following the signature of the agreement, Neville Chamberlain gave his infamous 'peace for our time' speech to the British media, but the German promises proved to be no more than a manoeuvre to buy time while Hitler planned the invasion of Poland. On 31 March

1939, Neville Chamberlain declared Great Britain and France's support of Poland, and on 6 April 1939 Britain entered into a mutual assistance pact with Poland, pledging military aid if the independence of the country should be threatened. This was no deterrent to Hitler's territorial ambitions, and Poland was invaded on 1 September. Britain and France sent Hitler an ultimatum, demanding that he withdraw his troops, or they would declare war on Germany. The ultimatum was brazenly disregarded and the Germans continued their advance. Britain and France declared war on 3 September, and, just over twenty years after the cessation of World War I, Europe was plunged once more into conflict.

Norway had maintained a neutral stance in World War I and expected to be able to do so again; in fact, immediately after the outbreak of war, Norway, Denmark, Sweden and Finland all declared their neutrality. The Norwegian military was mobilised to protect the country's national borders and defend its neutrality, but the defence forces were small and their equipment was badly in need of modernisation. In 1939 the Royal Norwegian Navy had only 62 vessels, 43 of which dated back to before 1918. With a 2,650-kilometre-long seaboard to the west and a shared border, stretching some 1,600 kilometres, with neutral Sweden to the east, the Norwegian forces were ill-equipped for their task.

The Norwegian Navy needed to be expanded rapidly, and naval command looked to the country's large fishing and merchant fleets for the most suitable vessels to be taken into naval service. In Honningsvåg a likely candidate was the whaler *Thorodd*, which had been built in America as a steam-driven escort trawler for the French Navy. However, *Fleurus*, as she was originally named, did not enter service with the French Navy until August 1919, too late for service in World War I. She was sold and subsequently changed hands a number of times.

In 1924 she was converted to a cargo and passenger vessel, and a mail boat, for service between the Falkland Islands and the British and Norwegian whaling stations on South Georgia Island in the Antarctic. In 1935 she was bought by the Honningsvåg whaling company, A/V Thorodd, and underwent conversion to a whale catcher. She was then renamed *Thorodd*. Photographs of the time show a vessel that by today's standards was no beauty. She was a sizeable ship, 46 metres in length, with a beam of 7.7 metres, and weighing 450 tonnes. Steel-hulled, blunt-bowed and with a somewhat top-heavy superstructure, her bluff lines were utilitarian rather than streamlined, and after twenty years of working in harsh environments she was a rather tired old whaling ship.

By the outbreak of the war, whaling was a dying occupation. Mineral oils had replaced the valuable whale oils that previously had been essential ingredients in lubricants, lamp oil, cooking, cosmetics and many other products. Synthetic plastics had largely removed the need for whale bone, and the main commercial value remained in whale meat. Over-hunting had depleted whale stocks in Arctic waters, and *Thorodd* was obliged to make long trips to the South Atlantic Ocean to find her quarry.

Thorodd reverted to her original naval function when she was hired by the Norwegian Navy on 19 October 1939, 46 days after the outbreak of the war. Erling Hafto's past naval service, his continued association with the sea, the responsibility and experience that he had gained from his post of harbour-master and the fact that he was on the spot and immediately available marked him out as the ideal choice to take over her command. Even if he had not remained on the naval reserve list, his subsequent actions leave little doubt that he would have volunteered for service as soon as he saw the threat to his country.

In spite of the previous courtesy title of 'captain' given to him as harbour-master, Erling Hafto rejoined the navy as a lieutenant, which was the rank normally assigned to commanders of coastal patrol boats. Not long into the war, Erling's many qualities marked him out for promotion, and he ended the war as an *orlogskaptein* or commander. By custom, however, the commander of any vessel large or small is known as the captain, and his crew would have addressed him by this title. He has been referred to as Captain Hafto in previous accounts, and for simplicity and consistency he is referred to in this way hereafter.

Captain Hafto's first task was to engage a crew. He was 39 years old now, and commanded considerable respect in the community. There is no record of how many of *Thorodd*'s whaling crew volunteered to serve with him, but he had no difficulty in finding other crew members from the numbers of suitable seagoing men on Magerøya, eager to play their part in Norway's defence.

Captain Hafto took his new command to Hammerfest, a naval base about eight hours steaming from Honningsvåg, and *Thorodd* was hurriedly fitted out for coastal protection duties. An early step in *Thorodd*'s conversion was the removal of her bow-mounted whaling harpoon gun, and she was fitted with a 20-mm Oerlikon anti-aircraft cannon as her main armour. This Swiss-designed and manufactured weapon first saw service in World War I, and with later developments it became the most widely used and successful anti-aircraft gun of World War II. The Oerlikon revolutionised anti-aircraft warfare and the Norwegian Navy led the British and other Allied navies in ordering it. It was a formidable weapon with a rate of fire of 300 rounds per minute, and it provided Allied sailors with some of their best protection against enemy attack, thereby saving men's lives. *Thorodd*'s gun was fitted on a raised platform at the bow, allowing the weapon to be rotated through 360 degrees, and the gunner controlled it by a pair of shoulder crutches which he leant into. Apart from the Oerlikon cannon, the only other weapons on board were an old Krag-Jørgensen rifle and Captain Hafto's 11-mm automatic pistol.

Thorodd was now a ship of the Kongelige Norske Marine, the Royal Norwegian Navy. After being formally inducted into the navy and issued with uniform, the crew were introduced to a new routine and regime. The informality of life on board a whaler was exchanged for naval discipline and a period of intense training in the short time available to convert *Thorodd* to her new rôle. Captain Hafto's initial job was to galvanise this vengeful group of young Norse fishermen into a cohesive crew of disciplined naval fighters. The men's inherent sea skills foreshortened some of this training, but they still had to be introduced to new procedures and tactics, as well as techniques of naval communication, gunnery and weapon-handling, 'square-bashing' and other basic military drills. The ship took part in trials and exercises along with other units to familiarise the crew with the new procedures and with equipment such as ALDIS signalling.

Not every member of the crew was recruited locally. Alf N. Thomassen from Sandnes in southern Norway was amongst those keen to volunteer for service. After induction and basic training at the main naval recruiting base at Horten, near Oslo, he was drafted a long way from his home to the patrol vessel

Thorodd in the far north of the country. When he received his posting, he asked his superior officer, 'What kind of ship is that?'

'The finest ship in the navy!' was the confident reply.

He was therefore taken aback and felt somewhat deceived when he first reported for duty on board the battered whaler. So urgent had it been to get her back to sea to carry out her new duties that there had not been time to paint her the regulation battleship-grey, and she seemed to him to be very inadequately armed. Among the first of the crew to greet him as he stepped on board was the unexpected figure of Bamse. In traditional seafaring countries like Norway sea dogs are less unusual on board ships than in other nations, but Bamse was unique amongst ships' mascots because of his size. However, despite his initial surprise, Alf found Bamse's benign presence helpful in breaking the ice between himself and the established crew.

It had been Halldis Hafto who had settled the matter of Bamse's future when Erling took over command of *Thorodd*. She had been faced with the prospect of her husband returning to sea in the uncertain conditions of war and being left on her own to care for their four young children. The added responsibility of looking after the now fully grown family pet was daunting, given his size and enormous appetite, and the solution had been clear. 'Take Bamse with you,' she had pleaded. 'The children are more than enough for me to look after.'

So Bamse joined the navy and went to sea and, later, to war. There is now no record of his service number but the likely rank given him by the crew was *skipshunden* or ship's dog. It is uncertain whether higher command knew of his presence on the ship at this point, for his position on board was not to be formalised until 9 February 1940, when he was officially entered onto the ship's muster roll; this was probably done to ensure that proper canine rations were requisitioned for him.

With her inelegant looks and an unconventional crew member, *Thorodd* entered the war as a fighting ship of dubious provenance. Life on board, however, was increasingly agreeable for Alf Thomassen; the atmosphere was congenial and friendly, and discipline was reasonably relaxed. The captain's dog acted as if he owned the vessel and inspired camaraderie amongst all on board. Alf began to think that perhaps he had joined 'the finest ship in the navy' after all.

After her fitting-out and crew training were completed around the end of 1939, *Thorodd* was deployed on active service to No. 3 Sea Defence District (3 SFD). There were three districts encompassing the south (No. 1), the central (No. 2) and the northern (No. 3) sectors of Norway's seaboard. No. 3 Sea Defence District was a vast area of sea, islands and fjords, extending 800 kilometres from the Lofoten Islands to the North Cape. Its headquarters were at Tromsø, which, later on in the war, was to be the focus of much attention with the sinking of the German battleship, the *Tirpitz*. The Royal Norwegian Navy numbered in the region of 130 ships by this time, and they must have been considerably stretched in patrolling the whole of the coastline. *Thorodd's* main activity was escorting convoys to and from Narvik, about three quarters of the way up Norway's west coast. She was also on the lookout for covert enemy mine-laying operations and air and sea incursions.

Aside from his military responsibilities, Captain Hafto had the additional concern of Bamse's distinctly un-naval needs to take into account. It is known that a sheltered spot was found on *Thorodd's* upper deck, where a large wicker basket was secured for Bamse to rest in during the daytime if weather permitted. Below

decks, a broom cupboard was cleared and allocated to him as
his personal cabin, where he could retreat in bad weather. The
winter of 1939–40 was stormy and bitterly cold in the northern
waters. The men felt as though they would freeze to death, and
although Bamse fared better against the cold in his natural fur
coat, he disliked rough seas and suffered badly from sea sickness.
'I won't forget one very stormy night when I suddenly woke up
with a dog's wet nose in my face!' recalled Alf Thomassen. 'Poor
old Bamse wanted a bit of comfort!' Later in the war, if they
could, the crew left him on shore whenever the weather forecast
threatened wild weather.

The Norwegians' assumption that their neutrality would be
respected may now seem ingenuous, but at the time there was
general public and political support for the belief that Norway
should stay out of the war. Surprisingly, on the very grounds of
its neutrality, the nation attempted to keep trading with both
Britain and Germany, but the situation became increasingly
precarious. In December 1939 three British iron-ore ships were
torpedoed and sunk by German U-boats in Norwegian waters.
Lesser incidents happened quite frequently. In February 1940,
British marines entered Jøssingfjord and raided the German
tanker *Altmark* in order to liberate British prisoners being held
on board. Norway found itself a pawn at the centre of a great
game as both Germany and Great Britain sought control of
the country.

Norway's strategic position had been noted by both the
German High Command and the Allies as potentially vital to
their respective war efforts. For many years before the outbreak

of war, Germany had imported half of its iron-ore requirements, some 6 million tonnes annually, which it bought from Sweden. It was transported by land across Norway to the ice-free port of Narvik, where it was loaded onto ore carriers and shipped to Germany. Germany could not afford to lose so large a proportion of this material, essential for its war-machine and heavy industry, and it knew it must preserve its year-round access to Narvik. Norwegian neutrality notwithstanding, Great Britain and the Allies were not prepared to allow the iron ore, which would be used for the manufacture of ships, planes, bombs and tanks destined to attack their forces, to peacefully steam past them on its way to the German armament factories.

More importantly, both sides knew that the control of Norway and its coast was essential to dominance of the North Atlantic. German success in this region could bring Britain to its knees, while Allied success would deny Germany its vital iron ore and access to the northern ports and airfields from which its navy and air force could harass the important Russian convoys. During the winters of World War I, the German surface fleet had been ice-bound in the Baltic Sea, and the experience was still fresh in the German naval memory. Norwegian ports and bases, however, would offer their submarines year-round access to the North Sea and the Atlantic Ocean, and the deep fjord waters would provide protection and concealment for their warships.

In December 1939, Hitler ordered his trusted long-time ally General Alfred Jodl, who was chief of the operations staff in the Wehrmacht and in charge of the development of strategic and operational plans, to find an excuse to breach Norway's neutrality and plan for its invasion. With the Allies' corresponding interest in keeping Norway under their influence, it was not long before both sides felt they had powerful reasons to enter Norwegian soil.

General Jodl's plan, codenamed Operation Weserübung, was to occupy Norway and also Denmark, with which it shared a common boundary. There was the prospect of strong counter-measures from Britain, including rumours that the British were holding secret talks with the Norwegian government to permit the occupation of Norway by Allied troops. It was at this point that Vidkun Quisling, whose name was to become synonymous with betrayal, stepped onto history's stage. He was leader of the Norwegian Nasjonal Samling or National Unity Party, which had parallel sympathies with the German Nazi Party, and he persuaded the Nazis that there was strong support amongst ordinary Norwegians for a German occupation of their country.

Germany commenced Operation Weserübung on 9 April 1940, and the day was named Wesertag. The operation represented a new strategy in military planning as it was the first major combined army, navy and air force operation of the twentieth century carried out by any country. A full army corps was assembled, comprising six divisions supported by practically the whole German naval fleet and a thousand aircraft. The plan was to simultaneously invade Norway and Denmark with lightning speed and overpowering force, capturing the kings of both countries to assure immediate surrender. Denmark was not as strategically important to Germany's war plans as Norway, but it was Germany's border neighbour and could be used as a staging post for an attack by Germany's enemies. Denmark's small army stood little chance against the highly trained invading German troops, but it did put up a resistance and suffered several dozen fatalities. However, faced with the threat of mass bombing of the civilian population by the Luftwaffe, the Danish government took the view, wisely, that surrender was the greater part of valour and capitulated within hours.

Norway, however, presented a different challenge. Its people, its parliament and King Haakon VII himself were not of a mind to surrender without a struggle, and they put up a brave resistance in the face of overwhelming odds. The country's geography presented the invading forces with particular logistical, strategic and tactical difficulties. The 2,650-kilometre-long coastline, indented with narrow, high-sided fjords, provided the German navy with secure deepwater anchorages for its capital ships, but, as experience showed, they could also be trapped and rendered ineffective or destroyed by attack from air and sea. Inland Norway is an untamed region of large coniferous forests, lakes and towering mountain peaks – a difficult terrain for invaders to negotiate, but an easy one for the defenders to use to their advantage, hindering the occupiers' movements through hit-and-run partisan resistance.

In April 1940 a hastily assembled expeditionary force of British, French and Polish troops was sent to aid the Norwegians. They were badly equipped and poorly supported, and, although they put up a gallant fight, they lacked experience in Arctic warfare against a superior, well-trained German force.

During the period after the invasion of 9 April 1940, *Thorodd* undertook a more active role and was involved in a number of engagements over the next 62 days before Norway was forced to capitulate. One of *Thorodd*'s duties at this time was transporting German prisoners of war. Judging by tales of his subsequent attitude to guard duty and efficiency as a guard dog, it is fair to surmise that Bamse would have been a firm, but intractable, jailer.

It was in this brief period of 62 days that Bamse established his reputation for being 'fearless in action' and 'steadfast under fire'. He did not cower below decks at the sound of gunfire, but instead sustained the crew's morale by remaining on deck throughout action, stationed at his usual place beside the Oerlikon gunner, and acting as a symbol of courage and inspiration for the frightened young sailors. He is said to have stood on the bow-gun platform 'facing the enemy, with his teeth bared'. Enemy fighter pilots must have questioned their eyesight, if not their sanity, as they came in for attack and met the intense stare of the gunner's canine mate blazing out from beneath a steel helmet, hackles erect on his back and tail straight out behind him, teeth bared and lips drawn back in a furious snarl – all classic signs of canine aggression. It is remarkable that Bamse never suffered the slightest injury during exchanges with the enemy. Nonetheless, there was very real danger, and so concerned were the crew for his safety that they had altered a standard-issue steel helmet to fit his head, with a chin-strap to keep it secure. He always wore this when *Thorodd* went into action. A photograph of him wearing his helmet and posing with some of the crew on the aft deck of *Thorodd* was widely circulated later, adding to his growing reputation as a dog of war.

Dr Willie Nilsen, now a consultant psychiatrist in Harstad, heard stories about Bamse from his father, who served on *Thorodd* later in the war. 'We speak about the men,' he observed, 'but after all they were just boys. My father was old, he was 33; most were in their late teens and early twenties. They couldn't speak to their friends or anybody else about being afraid, or wanting to go home . . . or whatever. I'm quite sure Bamse was a good therapist for a large number of these boys.'

Very much later, Vigdis Hafto echoed his thoughts: 'These were indeed very frightening times for young sailors, so if you have a dog to talk to, like the men had on *Thorodd*, they were lucky, I think. There he was, a good friend, who would understand and not laugh if a tear fell to the floor. If Bamse had been able to speak in words, I'm sure he would have told a lot of things, but he just understood and comforted.'

Aboard *Thorodd*, Bamse was in his adopted element, with his adopted family. He, of course, had no concept of war or its consequences, although he would have been aware that familiar routines had changed. When he sniffed the bitter winds of uncertainty that bothered his shipmates he most likely thought only that they were in for another rough sail. He had proved himself highly adaptable, from home-based child-minder to ship's cabin dog; from land-based dog of all trades to seagoing gunner's mate; from family pet to ship's mascot; from captain's companion to crew's confidant. He had shown himself gentle with small children, but was defiant under cannon-fire from enemy fighter planes. If, as Willie Nilsen suggests, he was 'a good therapist', then his healing skills must have manifested themselves almost from the first exchange between *Thorodd* and the enemy. It all reinforced the perception that Bamse was no ordinary dog.

By the end of May, the struggle to defend Norway was nearly over, and resistance in the south had been overcome. King Haakon VII and his government had to move northwards and on one occasion they were forced to take cover in the forest around Tromsø, so close was the enemy. Hitler dearly wanted to capture the Norwegian king because of the political and emotional authority he would gain from holding so important and symbolic a hostage. He would have had the means of installing a sham, but constitutionally legitimate, puppet government, and could have expected more cooperation from the Norwegian people.

Naval battles and some Allied successes continued around Narvik, but after disastrous setbacks an early decision was taken by the Allies to withdraw from Norway. On 3 June the order was given to evacuate the Allied Forces, marking the end of one of the Allies' least notable operations. At the same time as these events, the British Expeditionary Force in France was retreating towards Dunkirk, where more than 345,000 troops were evacuated from the beaches to escape the advancing German army sweeping through western Europe.

The Norwegian forces fought on, but the sheer numbers of the invading troops and their superior training and equipment made long-term resistance unsustainable. On 7 June 1940, after heavy fighting involving losses of ships and men on both sides, all personnel of the Royal Norwegian Navy were ordered to save their ships and make good their escape to Britain in whatever way they could.

The monarch, especially in times of war, is the embodiment of the nation, as Britain, with its own monarch, was profoundly aware. The British government, therefore, was quick to extend the hand of friendship to King Haakon, and the British navy mounted a top-secret operation to save him. The heavy cruiser HMS *Devonshire* had been ordered to Tromsø Fjord, arriving on 7 June. That same day the tall figure of King Haakon and the rest of the royal family, accompanied by members of the government and diplomats of other Allied nations, climbed the gangplank. They also managed to spirit away with them almost the entire Norwegian gold reserves, which would be used to finance the government in exile. They were met on board by Admiral John Cunningham, who had strict orders to maintain radio silence and not to deviate in any respect from the mission entrusted to him. Despite being chased out of their homes and their own country, Norway's royal family and government took with them the spirit and will of their country's people; they were resolved to set up a Norwegian government in exile and determined to rattle the bars of the cage which the Germans had thrown round their country.

Captain Hafto was one of only 13 ship commanders from the navy of 130 vessels who was in a position to obey the order to follow the king to Britain. The rest of the Norwegian fleet had been captured, sunk or damaged. Nine of the survivors had fallen back to the northern sector and been ordered to proceed with all speed to Tromsø Fjord to provide cover and escort for HMS *Devonshire*. They were a motley assortment of battle-weary and scarred vessels, including the submarine *B1*, two fishery-protection vessels, a captured German armed trawler and five armed patrol vessels. One of the patrol vessels, the Norwegian Royal Yacht *Heimdal*, dated back to the 19th century; in spite of her age, she had been actively engaged during the fighting. She escaped to Scotland and spent the rest of the war at Port Edgar on the Firth of Forth. The other four patrol vessels *Thorodd*, *Nordhav II*, *Bortind* and *Syrian* would form a minesweeper squadron based in Dundee and stay together for most of the rest of the war.

Devonshire wasted no time once her passengers had boarded and the gold was stowed securely. She slipped her moorings and headed out in the half light of a Norwegian summer's night into the hostile Norwegian Sea, where German warships were known to be operating. The flotilla of small Norwegian ships was ordered to accompany *Devonshire* as far as possible and then scatter and make their own way to Scotland. With a top speed of 34 knots, *Devonshire* quickly left the straggling Norwegian flotilla behind and, avoiding detection, skirted round the Shetland Islands and the west of Scotland, safely landing her important passengers at Greenock, west of Glasgow on the River Clyde, on 10 June 1940. Five years later, on the anniversary of the evacuation, *Devonshire* was to return in triumph to Norway, escorting HMS *Norfolk*, which had been given the honour of returning King Haakon to his country.

Heimdal and *Thorodd*, with Bamse aboard, cast off their moorings at the same time, 0355 hours on 8 June. Even at this late stage, young Norwegians were clamouring to be taken aboard the small ships of the flotilla. They too wanted to escape and join the Free Norwegian Forces in Britain and they jumped at any chance to be taken on board a ship. At the last moment, *Thorodd* took on an extra four men, one of whom, Albert Andersen, was later to form a particularly close bond with Bamse.

The feelings of the departing sailors can only be imagined – they were in tactical retreat, taking with them possibly only what belongings they had been able to snatch when the order to sail to Britain was given. They were leaving behind them families, school friends, girlfriends and jobs. For all they knew, they might never see any of them again, or never be able to return home. Those who left without even photos of their loved ones had only their memories to sustain them in the quiet times of reflection and recall. It takes courage to leave behind all that is familiar and sail into an uncertain future. These young men had already endured the fear, stress and hardship of 62 days of action on a ship with only meagre defences, ill-suited for warfare. They would have been only too well aware of the power of the enemy they faced, and, until they were formally ordered to retreat, had been prepared to fight to the last shell and lay down their lives. Despite their retreat, however, it is clear that they did not regard themselves as in hopeless flight; they sailed away to join the common battle, with a determination to return to face the aggressors and win back their country's freedom.

4

Clearing the Decks

Although their future was now uncertain, Captain Hafto and the crew of *Thorodd* did at least have a degree of control over their present. For the most part they were whalers and fishermen, sailors accustomed to the vagaries of the seas and the weather, and they were in their natural element on board a boat that was familiar to most of them. Consequently they worked together well as a crew, and, of course, their spirits were buoyed up by the genial and caring presence of ship's mascot Bamse.

As *Devonshire*'s stern sped swiftly westward, her wake dissipating into an ever-widening 'V', there was no time for the watchers on *Thorodd* to be looking back to Norway. *Thorodd* had a likely maximum speed of between 12 and 15 knots, and in the state of war that existed between the two countries she was fair game for any German warship with which she came into contact. She would easily have been outpaced by a modern vessel, and her Oerlikon cannon was no match against a larger ship's armoury, so her immediate objective was to get away from home waters as rapidly as possible and make her way to Scotland.

In much the same way that Scotland's west coast is protected by the island chains of the Inner and Outer Hebrides, so Norway's coast off Tromsø is protected by the Lofoten Islands, which provide a measure of cover for a small ship wanting to remain undetected for as long as possible. Other than *Thorodd*'s, little is known of the courses the remaining ships set for Scotland; in any case, each crew would have decided this for themselves. None of the flotilla appears to have known that the Royal Navy had been busy laying mines in the sea lanes around the Lofoten Islands to discourage German naval activity and, with luck, destroy enemy shipping. *Devonshire*, with her royal passenger on board, must have been aware of the situation and been given a safe course to plot, but, whether for security reasons or as a result simply of the chaos of war, this information was either poorly communicated or did not reach the other ships at all.

Olav August Johan Nilsen (the father of psychiatrist Dr Willie Nilsen) was a coastal pilot based in Harstad. He had boarded the armed patrol vessel *Syrian*, which was another ship in the small fleet assembled near Tromsø, to escort HMS *Devonshire* out of Norwegian waters. He did not know it, but this was *Syrian*'s final homeland duty, and, once her task was fulfilled, her orders were to make an immediate getaway; her next port of call would be anything up to 1,600 kilometres away. As a civilian pilot, Olav was faced with a dilemma. He had boarded *Syrian* that morning expecting to carry out his piloting duties and return to port as normal. It was only when he was far from shore without so much as a toothbrush to his name, and having said only perfunctory farewells to his family, that he realised that the pilot boat had returned to Harstad without him. *Syrian*'s captain very fairly offered him the choice of being put ashore at a suitable safe place or sailing with *Syrian* to Scotland to fight the war from there.

He was a single man, and his concerns were for his parents and the rest of his family. Olav considered the offer and, with measured irony, enquired, 'The Germans don't eat people, do they, Captain?' On the reassurance that they did not and that his family was at least safe from that fate, he chose to stay with

Syrian and was immediately made navigation officer. His first
duty was to set a course away from Norway (she in fact sailed
to Scapa Flow in Orkney). According to his son Willie, he
discovered only much later, and apparently to his great distress
when he thought of the possible consequences, that he had
taken *Syrian* through the middle of one of the recently seeded
and undisclosed British minefields. In the circumstances, it
was remarkably fortunate that Olav Nilsen and *Syrian* (which
he subsequently rose to command), *Thorodd* and the rest of the
escaping remnants of the Norwegian Navy were all to make safe
passage to their several destinations in Scotland.

Having bidden farewell to HMS *Devonshire*, Captain Hafto
turned *Thorodd*'s steering wheel to steam south. The 1,450-
kilometre crossing to Scotland was stormy but otherwise
uneventful, and on 12 June *Thorodd* sailed into Lerwick, principal
town and port of the Shetland Islands, the archipelago of islands
at the northern extremity of the United Kingdom. The islands
are nearer to the Arctic Circle than to London and at the same
latitude as the large Norwegian town of Bergen. The sense of
relief amongst *Thorodd*'s crew when they tied up safely at Lerwick
may well have conveyed itself to Bamse, just as he probably sensed
their feelings of apprehension about unseen or imagined dangers
facing them during the five days and nights of the crossing.

The Royal Yacht *Heimdal*, which had left Tromsø at the same
time as *Thorodd,* was much slower due to her age and arrived
at Lerwick on 14 June.

Norman Lawrance was a nine-year-old schoolboy growing up in
Lerwick at the outbreak of World War II. These were exciting

times for a young boy with the sole ambition of going to sea when he grew up. Shetland was too far north for the horrors of war to make much of an impression on Norman, but he remembers the build-up of seagoing traffic at Lerwick Harbour, particularly fishing boats and other small craft escaping from the German threat. Initially, although this soon changed, there were no security measures around the harbour; he and his gang of friends from the Central School, drawn by the increasing naval activity, came and went as they pleased, haunting the area in their free time.

The Orkney and Shetland Islands were colonised by Norway in the ninth century and became a Norwegian province. Although they both subsequently returned to the Scottish crown, they have retained strong cultural and historical links with their former overlord, for the Shetlands are where Scotland meets Scandinavia and the North Sea salutes the Atlantic Ocean. Lerwick is the hub of a natural maritime crossroads for trading and provisioning and its harbour is a refuge from storms for passing ships. Ever since the Vikings sailed out on their plundering voyages, the Norskies (the Shetlanders' affectionate nickname for their Norwegian neighbours) have regarded the islands as a safe haven, and never more so than after the German invasion.

After Norway fell, and particularly after the two great sea battles of Narvik in 1940, Lerwick was the main centre of operations for the British naval campaign across the North Sea. Norman remembers inspecting the Clyde-built E-class destroyer HMS *Eclipse*, which had been hit by a bomb and badly damaged off Norway on 11 April 1940, and the sloop HMS *Pelican*, which was nearly crippled during an air attack off the Scottish coast some days later. Both ships made it to Lerwick and were patched up well enough to limp south to be properly repaired.

The naval and military build-up accelerated and the harbour became a restricted zone, with barbed wire erected around the whole perimeter. It proved to be only a minor inconvenience for slim lads like Norman, who found spots where they could squeeze below it, although the patches on their trousers showed just how tight a squeeze it sometimes was!

Norman's family lived at the south end of Lerwick on an elevated peninsula, known as Twageos (after the two sea inlets, or *geos*, on either side of it), overlooking the south end of one of the world's great natural harbours, the Sound of Bressay, which separates mainland Shetland from the island of Bressay. One day, Norman was off school with mumps. Gazing from his bedroom window, he saw six distant planes sweeping up the Sound from the south. Against his mother's bidding, he ran outside and, from the black crosses painted on their fuselages, identified them as German Heinkel bombers. So close to sea level were they flying that Norman could see the faces of the pilots. He sprang into imaginary action, blazing away with his imaginary machine-gun. Several moments later, he heard the chatter of real machine-guns and learned that they had shot up and sunk a Sunderland flying boat moored at the top of the harbour. This was the first enemy attack of the war on any military installation in Shetland.

Large numbers of Norwegians had escaped to Britain and joined the Free Forces, and many were posted to Shetland, where the Norwegian Navy had a squadron of MTBs (motor torpedo boats), two submarines and a Catalina flying boat. This coincided with a rapid influx of British forces to protect the islands and prevent them being used as a stepping-stone for a German invasion of mainland Scotland. HMS *Coventry*, the C-class anti-aircraft cruiser, was sent to Shetland following the sinking of the Sunderland flying boat, and Sumburgh was developed as an RAF station. Anti-aircraft defence posts were built at strategic points all over the islands and land-based torpedo tubes were sited on the beach at The Knab, a rocky promontory below Norman Lawrance's house.

This activity attracted regular attention from the Germans, who flew many reconnaissance sorties in particular, but some bombing raids too, over the islands. They attacked Scottish lighthouses, shooting out the lights, and a lighthouse keeper's wife was killed on Fair Isle. One bombing raid on the main island of Shetland was frustrated by heavy anti-aircraft fire, and the escaping pilots jettisoned their bombs in order to gain more speed. The bombs fell on moorland, and an unfortunate rabbit was the sole casualty, inspiring the popular wartime Flanagan and Allan song 'Run Rabbit Run'.

Sent on an errand one day by his mother, Norman met a member of his school playground gang who reported an unusual arrival of a 'wee black Norskie', which had moored up at the breakwater beside the lifeboat station at the harbour. Apparently 'a great big dog' was on board, and that caught Norman's imagination. Forgetting the errand, he ran to the boat, which was grounded on mud as the tide was out. Peering down from the quay, Norman met the soulful gaze of the biggest dog he had ever seen – and a breed he didn't recognise – sitting alone on the deck. Propping up the harbour wall were the Pierhead Council 'auld sauts' (old salts), who had gathered to see the new arrival. These retired seamen were the information exchange at the harbour and missed little of what went on. Norman remembers one of them, who wore an old cheese-cutter cap and was clearly the council joker, teasing him by saying, 'Look at that, the Norskies are even bringing across their ponies.' After a few moments of fun, another one of the old boys cleared matters up, explaining that the dog was a St Bernard. The wee black boat was of course *Thorodd*, and the dog was Bamse, who had made his landfall in Scotland and was ready to fight his war.

Norman Lawrance fulfilled his ambition to go to sea and rose to become a captain in the Merchant Navy, later retiring to Montrose. He had forgotten this childhood incident with the big dog, until 65 years after the event when publicity surrounding the plan to erect a statue to Bamse at Montrose harbour threw a switch in his brain, causing him to have vivid flashbacks about the episode. It is once more testament to Bamse's extraordinary presence that after more than half a century Norman Lawrance should recall with such clarity the single occasion that he briefly saw the dog.

Meanwhile, after racing off with King Haakon, HMS *Devonshire* had headed for the port of Clydebank, several kilometres downriver from Glasgow on the west coast of Scotland, which at the time was at the height of its shipbuilding activities producing warships. Her course took her round Cape Wrath, the most northwesterly tip of mainland Scotland, which surprisingly did not get its name from the stormy seas which sometimes rage around it. The wild-sounding name in fact derives from a Norse word meaning 'turning point', for the headland is on what had been a busy Viking sea route, and it was here, on their homeward journeys after their raiding excursions, that the Norsemen turned their longships' bows to head for home and safety. For King Haakon, the contemporary embodiment of his ancestral past, it was a turning point too, but one no doubt heavy with a mix of emotions very different to those of his ancestors, for his journey was taking him in the opposite direction, away from his country.

It shows the relative difference in the speed of the two ships that HMS *Devonshire* arrived in the River Clyde on 10 June, two days ahead of *Thorodd*'s arrival in Lerwick, which was roughly 700 kilometres closer to the ships' departure point.

Thorodd stayed in Shetland only long enough for Captain Hafto to report the boat's arrival to the British naval authorities and to receive orders about where he should proceed. On 15 June *Thorodd* cast off from her mooring, sailed out of Lerwick and on 17 June arrived in Port Edgar, which lies in the shadow of the distinctive Forth Rail Bridge, on the south bank of the Firth of Forth. Later that day, *Heimdal* sailed in and moored up alongside. The port had been designated as the main assembly point for Norwegian naval vessels that had escaped after the fall of their country, and *Thorodd* and *Heimdal* were amongst the first Norwegian boats to arrive. A disparate fleet of other fishing and whaling boats that were to be converted into naval service vessels joined them. *Heimdal* transferred to the Norwegian Rosyth naval section on 30 June and became the Norwegian command and depot ship.

Within weeks the collection of little ships at Port Edgar was joined by a straggle of men who had managed to escape from Norway at around the same time as King Haakon and the government. Some had hitched a lift on one or other of the departing navy ships. Others, young women as well as men, sought freedom on fishing boats and even smaller craft, some sailing and even rowing the shortest route (some 400 kilometres) between Norway and Shetland. Amongst the many dramatic escape stories are those of Bjørn Hagen and Herman Eilertsen, who came to Scotland and subsequently joined the Norwegian minesweepers, becoming shipmates of Bamse.

Bjørn Hagen arrived at Port Edgar on 20 June 1940, having been captured and recaptured several times before he finally found a way out of Norway. He had an exciting escape from Narvik at the beginning of the month amidst the chaos that prevailed at the time of the collapse of resistance. He was a merchant seaman and had returned home from his last voyage when the threat from Germany was becoming more acute. He joined the Royal Norwegian Navy just before Germany invaded and a week later was on the coastal defence battleship KNM *Eidsvold*, which, after a short stand-off, was hit by four torpedoes from the German destroyer *Wilhelm Heidkamp*. He was amongst the few survivors and was picked up by the German ship, but decided to jump overboard to make his escape. After this second spell in the water, he was pulled out by the Germans again and, suffering from hypothermia, was sent to hospital in Narvik.

That night there was a bombing raid. Bjørn and another of the surviving sailors took advantage of the confusion to escape and hide in the nurse's quarters. They found some Red Cross uniforms, which they put on, deciding that the best way of avoiding being found was to stay in the hospital where no one would think of looking for them. Their plan was successful and they avoided detection for some weeks. They then went into hiding until the beginning of June, when they learned that young Norwegians like them were escaping to Britain to continue the fight. They joined a company of 21 young men, military and civilians, who were keen to get away, and attempted to requisition a Norwegian fishing boat whose skipper was uncooperative and tried to make off without them. A burst of machine-gun fire across his bows overcame his reluctance and the men boarded. They escaped from Narvik and took a course for the Faeroe Islands, nearly 1,600 kilometres to the southwest. On arrival they were directed on to Port Edgar. Already an enlisted member of the navy, Bjørn was ordered to join the crew of *Thorodd*, which had arrived the week before.

Herman Eilertsen came from fishing stock and grew up in Øygarden, on an island seaward of Bergen. He too was a merchant seaman and when war broke out he was far from home on a Norwegian South America Line ship. When he returned home, Norway had been overrun by the Nazis. Like many of his age who refused to work for or collaborate with the Germans, he found himself rejected by those Norwegians who did, and, aged 19, he burned with the desire to escape to Britain to fight with the Free Norwegians. On Sunday 16 March 1941, he and four other young men 'borrowed' a 10-metre half-decked motor fishing boat. Leaving Øygarden at 2300 hours, they crossed the 400 kilometres of open sea to Lerwick, arriving during the morning of Tuesday 18 March. He remembers the voyage clearly: 'We were incredibly lucky with the weather at that time of year. The sea was calm, and there was a fog to hide us from the Germans.'

On arrival at Lerwick, they were sent to an assembly point for Norwegians who had made similar hazardous crossings. After refuelling and provisioning they were ordered to sail south to Buckie, a fishing port on the Moray Firth north of Aberdeen, and a further 400-kilometre journey away in the open boat. They were asked to take with them as passengers six other refugees, including two girls. At Buckie they caught a train to London, where Herman made his way to the Norwegian Admiralty and enlisted in the navy. As soon as the formalities were completed and he had been issued with his uniform, he found himself on a train on his way back to Scotland. He was posted to the minesweeper training school at Port Edgar, where his quarters were unexpectedly regal, as his berth was a cabin on the Royal Yacht *Heimdal*! His enthusiasm to play his part in the war and take the fight back to the Nazis was tempered, though, by the standing naval black humour directed at new arrivals at the start of their six weeks' training: 'You'll only last a fortnight on a minesweeper!' he was told.

The onshore naval command at Port Edgar was known as HMS *Lochinvar*. It became the permanent headquarters of the Royal Norwegian Navy in Scotland for the rest of the war, and King Haakon was given offices there for use whenever he was in Scotland. HMS *Lochinvar* was under the control and command of the much larger HMS *Cochrane* at HM Dockyard across the river at Rosyth. HMS *Lochinvar* had dockyard fabrication and repair facilities, and it was here that *Thorodd* and the other Norwegian vessels were fitted out for their new wartime roles.

The Royal Navy's only minesweeping training school during the war was also located at HMS *Lochinvar,* and as *Thorodd* was chosen for conversion to a minesweeper, crew and ship could be worked up together. She was out of commission for five and a half months, from 1 August 1940 until 10 February 1941, while the work was completed.

Shore establishments are referred to by sailors as 'stone frigates', and it was from his new stone kennel that the next phase of Bamse's story began. HMS *Lochinvar* took on a secondary role as Bamse's training ground, providing him with an introduction to his new life in Scotland. On board *Thorodd*, things remained by and large the same, but there were cultural challenges and social adjustments for Bamse to make on shore.

In Lerwick, there was much that was familiar to Bamse:

island life, the island people and the Scandinavian intonation in their speech, the familiarity of routine on board ship and the availability of fresh fish, for which he had acquired a taste. Life as a ship's dog had accustomed him to trips away from home, as well as tying up at distant ports where St Bernard dogs were as unexpected and noteworthy, as had been the case in Shetland.

Life ashore at Port Edgar, however, was very different – not just for Bamse, but for some of the crew members too, exposed for the first time to the comparative sophistication and refinement of wartime central Scotland. Bamse experienced a number of 'firsts' in the coming weeks for which nothing had prepared him, but which he accepted with his usual composure. Trusting completely in his shipmates' judgement, he climbed on board his first bus, a form of transport that he quickly adapted to, according to later stories. He was also able to watch trains passing over the Forth Bridge, as there was a clear view of the bridge from *Thorodd*'s deck. It was not a long walk from the ship's berth to the local train stop at Dalmeny Junction at the south end of the bridge, and from here Bamse and his shipmates could board a train to Edinburgh, or travel north into Fife. He had to accustom himself to the local West Lothian dialect, and it would not be so very long until he had to acclimatise again to Dundee speech, but with his natural adaptability he took it all in his stride. For some of the younger crew members, whose life experience scarcely extended beyond Magerøya, all this was new to them too, and dog and sailors shared these first-time adventures with each other.

It is not known exactly when Bamse was introduced to beer, but he displayed a sailor's steady head for alcohol without his habits becoming too intemperate. It is unlikely it happened during the short Lerwick stopover, for during the war years, and in fact until the late 1940s, that town was almost completely dry as there were no public bars and alcohol could only be purchased at licensed grocers. If Bamse had tasted beer before leaving Norway, he must surely have thought he was in heaven when he first visited the pubs around Port Edgar and South Queensferry and sampled some of the local brews for which the area was noted.

Bamse regularly accompanied the crew to the pub and enjoyed his beer as much as any of them, but he had firm ideas about the company he chose to drink with. Mrs Nan Meyer was married to a Norwegian gunnery instructor, Clement Meyer, who was based at the Dumbarton Gunnery School, but was a frequent visitor to HMS *Lochinvar*. She has passed on a story about a pub cat which was sitting on the end of the bar counter when Bamse and his shipmates came in for a drink. Perhaps it was the cat's supercilious look as it gazed down on the dog, or perhaps it was sitting just where he wanted to be; in any event, Bamse was not happy. Rising up on his hind legs, he placed his paws on the bar counter and evaluated the situation. With a casual flick of one paw, he swept the offending cat right off the end of the bar to make room for himself and then waited patiently while the publican drew a pint into a bowl which was set down before him.

Over the period of his wartime service large numbers of Norwegian sailors came under Bamse's influence. *Thorodd* had a regular ship's complement of 18 to 20 crew, but there was a turnover of about 130 personnel over the whole period. Especially during the times of her two lengthy refits, trained specialists whose skills were not being usefully employed were transferred to operational duties and replacements were posted to *Thorodd*. As headquarters for the Royal Norwegian Navy, the

Port Edgar quays and barracks were thronged with Norwegian ships and sailors, and rang with familiar Norwegian voices. It is unimaginable that so companionable a dog as Bamse did not pay courtesy calls to other ships and make the acquaintance of their crews, or from time to time accept invitations to join them on a jaunt to the pub.

Sailors out on a pass were required to be back on board ship or in barracks by a specified hour and faced punishment if they failed to make the curfew deadline. During the Port Edgar months, Bamse developed one of his most remarkable abilities, his curfew patrol, which has frequently been greeted with disbelief and even derision, but has been too well corroborated over the succeeding years to be fiction. Towards closing time in the pub, when last orders were called, Bamse herded together his drinking mates and began to physically nudge them away from the bar and out of the premises, before heading them in the direction of their ship. This became a common sight whenever *Thorodd* berthed at Montrose later on in the war. If he had stayed on board while his mates were ashore drinking, he made sure he left the ship in time to reach the bar before it closed and the crew went seeking more drink when they were put out on the street. Lingering on the way back was not permitted, and older Montrosians still tell of seeing Bamse putting his shoulder to crewmen who were too slow and needed a bit of persuasion to 'get a shift on'.

There is no knowing what motivated him to introduce this social service, but it undoubtedly helped keep his shipmates out of trouble. Perhaps his time spent looking after the Hafto children gave him the idea that he was in charge of all his two-legged companions, and he extended his nanny-dog responsibilities to these bigger children, keeping them in order.

It has been suggested that he was given his main feed of the day last thing at night, and this was the incentive to get everyone back to the ship. A more likely explanation is that the last orders' bell became synchronised with his own internal time clock, and he knew that life ran more smoothly if the crew were back on board by a particular hour.

Despite his size, Bamse was essentially a gentle animal. He bore the noise and tumult of enemy action with equanimity, but he could not abide fights and brawling, especially in bars and public houses. According to one story, he was once hit over the head with a bottle by a drunken sailor, and the memory stuck in his subconscious, making him intolerant of violent drunkenness. He was certainly sternly effective in bringing such nonsense to a halt, though he was never aggressive – he did not need to be. It was enough for him to rise up on his hind legs to his full height of six feet and place his paws on the shoulders of one of the combatants for order to be restored. There are no stories indicating that his behaviour was resented, nor that anyone tried to fight back or retaliate.

Thorodd's crew, especially those who had witnessed Bamse's gallantry under fire during the 62-day war with Germany, were as protective of their mascot as he was of them. Bamse's reputation was very personal to *Thorodd* and her crew, and they did not miss an opportunity to talk and even boast about him. It was during the period at Port Edgar that Bamse's reputation began to spread laterally. He was already *Thorodd*'s beacon and mascot; he then became base mascot for HMS *Lochinvar*. Free Norwegian Navy servicemen passing through HMS *Lochinvar* came in contact with him or heard the stories about him, and this helped disseminate the word about his spirit, his caring nature and his quirky routines like the curfew patrol. Some stories inevitably verged on the apocryphal, but his conduct throughout the rest of his life only served to reinforce his positive reputation.

During a ship's refit, it is normal for at least a skeleton crew to remain on board for security reasons and to carry out duties such as guarding the gangway against unauthorised visitors. Bamse often took his turn along with the sailors and he must have been welcome company in the dark hours of a cold Scottish night. From time to time the guard left his post to go to the lavatory or sneak to the mess for a cup of coffee, and ordered Bamse to watch the gangway in his absence. Bamse took his duties seriously and stood with his forepaws on the top rung of the gangway, firmly denying all comers entry to *Thorodd* – whoever they were.

Former crew member Anders Petterøe tells a story of when he was on duty one evening with Bamse. In the course of his watch he needed to answer a call of nature. Leaving Bamse with the usual order to keep guard he slipped off to 'shed a tear for Nelson'. Moments later, Captain Erling Hafto tried to board his ship. Bamse took his place at the head of the gangplank and resolutely refused to allow his master, the captain of the ship, to come on board until Anders had returned to his post and ordered him to do so. Erling was extremely angry, and Anders describes how his language descended to a level of lower-deck fluency which was quite unrepeatable – at least to Norwegians, but perhaps much of its robustness was lost on any Scotsmen looking on!

This was the second time that Bamse had openly defied his

master. Erling Hafto had had to concede to the dog's authority when he prohibited his master from visiting his daughter Vigdis during her illness. Again, on this occasion, despite his anger he did not try to force a showdown with Bamse or attempt to push his way on board. The unanswered question is: how would Bamse have reacted had he done so?

Football became one of Bamse's great loves. He was a vocal spectator and, given the chance, an enthusiastic if unskilled participant, relying on brawn rather than brain. Doubtless at home in Honningsvåg he had played backyard games with the Hafto children and their friends, using rolled-up jumpers for goals, but he was introduced to the serious aspects of the beautiful game in the months at HMS *Lochinvar*, when the crew needed outlets for their excess energy. HMS *Lochinvar* Royal Navy Camp was built at the north end of the adjoining Wardie School's playing fields and what more likely than that the sailors played on the football pitch when it was not being used by the school children. When *Thorodd* later moved north to her base at Dundee, Bamse became a familiar figure on the touchline at football matches there and at Montrose.

Thorodd's refit lasted from 1 August 1940 until 10 February 1941, a total of five and a half months, in which time she was transformed. Comparison of photographs taken before and after her conversion shows that a new bridge, chart room and radio operator's cabin appear to have been added as a new upper level of accommodation. The captain's and senior officers' quarters comprised a middle level and at deck level itself there was a forward main mess room (above the engines for extra warmth), junior officers' accommodation and ordinary seamen's accommodation aft – too far away to benefit from the warmth.

Thorodd was described on several occasions as a 'rust bucket', which was not surprising after so many years' service in polar seas. Her dilapidated state explains why her conversion took so long; she presumably needed to be stripped out comprehensively and her basic services renewed before the real work of the refit could start. New signalling and communication equipment meeting Royal Navy specifications was installed, and improved light armour for defence fitted. Light machine-guns were positioned on either side of the bridge, and one photograph shows another machine-gun aft of the bridge. Her afterdeck was filled with the minesweeping gear, large drums of cable, winches, derricks, floats and the like. The new ASDIC (Anti-submarine Detection Investigation Committee) or sonar, which relied on echolocation to track underwater submarines, was also installed. From the audible 'pings', familiar to cinema audiences watching black-and-white naval wartime films, a skilled sonar operator could tell the range of an enemy submarine and whether it was approaching or moving away.

It was soon recognised that Erling Hafto's previous naval experience and skills were not being put to their best use while *Thorodd* was laid up at Port Edgar. On 9 September 1940, just weeks after *Thorodd*'s refit had begun, he was posted to command the Norwegian patrol vessel *Nordkapp* based at Hvalfordhur in Iceland, where his knowledge and experience of the Arctic seas were invaluable. It was generally assumed that as soon as Hitler had control of Norway his sights would be set on Iceland, which would consolidate Germany's stranglehold on the North Atlantic and be another nail in the coffin of the Atlantic convoys. Iceland had declared her neutrality at the outset of war but the occupation of Denmark and Norway showed that such pronouncements were disregarded by the German leadership.

To thwart further territorial ambitions Hitler might have had in the Arctic, the Allies decided to get there first, and latterly some 25,000 troops were stationed on Iceland, to the great relief of the islanders. Captain Hafto's new command was almost in the Arctic Circle and he relished the idea of taking on the enemy in familiar waters. However, his departure to Iceland sparked a near crisis.

Bamse had become essential to the morale and confidence of the whole crew, and the men depended on him for psychological support. It was natural for Captain Hafto to take his dog with him to his new command, and it was natural for the dog to accompany his master. However, as he completed his farewells to the crew and prepared to leave the ship the crew confronted him.

'My father came to the gangway with Bamse by his side, ready to leave,' explained Vigdis. 'One of the crew came forward and asked, "Is the commander taking Bamse with him?" "Yes, it is my dog and I shall take him with me," my father replied. "If that is so, we will not go out to sea," was the response.'

The brave soul who agreed to be spokesman was most likely Chief Engineer Anders Christian Larsen. There is a handsome photograph showing him seated with Bamse by his side, and he looks to be in his mid thirties to forties, so he would have been of an age with Erling Hafto. He was a senior officer and would not have been dismissed out of hand because there were bonds of friendship and respect between the two men.

Despite the captain's remonstrations, the men remained resolute in their demand and repeated their threat of disobedience if he took their mascot with him. Realising that the morale of the crew was critical, Captain Hafto agreed that Bamse should stay with *Thorodd* and become the responsibility of the new commander, but that he was on loan only and he would return for him after the war. Again it says much about the captain that he put the crew's interests before his own and his decision to leave Bamse must have heightened the poignancy of his departure from his ship.

Vigdis Hafto believes that her father kept in touch with *Thorodd*, receiving news of Bamse's exploits, and that he managed to see his dog briefly several times in the course of the war. If he had guessed that Bamse would not survive the war he might have been less exasperated by the crew's insubordination and taken a much more solicitous farewell of his family's dearly loved friend.

5

Tides of War

Eight months is a long time to wait for retribution, but *Thorodd*'s conversion to a minesweeper was finally complete, and she could join battle with the enemy. Lieutenant Reidar Cook Thovsen had assumed command shortly after Erling Hafto's transfer to Iceland, so the new captain and the ship's company had had time to familiarise themselves with each other and with their new tasks. And, of course, illuminating all their lives was the comforting and cheerful presence of Bamse. Whatever Lieutenant Thovsen might have known about Bamse's influence on the crew's confidence before he took command, he was obviously immediately charmed by the big dog and understood the value of his presence on board.

In early March 1941 *Thorodd* said farewell to HMS *Lochinvar* and, with a jubilant salute from her siren as she sailed beneath the Forth Rail Bridge, headed out of the broad firth of the River Forth and into the North Sea. If subsequent stories are anything to go by, Bamse was standing at the bow on the Oerlikon gun platform, sharing the all-Norwegian crew's elation and anticipation at being able, at last, to 'give it back' to the oppressive Nazis who had overrun their country. Their destination was the port of Dundee, 65 sea miles north, which occupied a deepwater position on the north bank of the River

Tay, downriver of the Tay Rail Bridge where the estuary starts to broaden.

Dundee's prosperity had long been built on 'the three Js' – jute, jam and journalism. By the start of the 20th century, if not earlier, it had grown into a true boomtown, so much so that neighbouring Broughty Ferry was described as the richest square mile in Europe because of the wealth of the Dundee jute barons and the splendour of their mansions. Coincidentally, the two towns were further interwoven by Broughty Ferry's historic links with the whaling industry, which had contributed to the explosion of the city's jute production in the previous century. The Ferry's whaling ships brought back whale oil, which was originally added to the jute fibres to make them more pliable and easier to weave. As production methods developed, however, the whale oil ceased to be used. Another historical footnote is that it was the insatiable demand for jute sacking to make defensive sandbags during the American Civil War of 1861 to 1865 which, more than any other factor, helped to establish Dundee as the world's jute manufacturing centre, ultimately being nicknamed 'Juteopolis'.

By the wartime 1940s, Dundee's output of jute (for jute sacking and carpet-backing, or burlap) was colossal. But India, where the hemp which provided the fibres from which jute is woven was grown, was fast developing its own jute industry and competing for the trade. That competition and the introduction, post war, of man-made fibres such as polypropylene spelled the end of the city's domination of the industry, and Dundee's last jute mill ceased production in 1999. Dundee was also the Home of Marmalade but, with the demise of the famous Keillor family who built the first marmalade factory in 1797, it is just a sweet memory now as there is no longer any marmalade or jam made in the city itself, although Mackays continue the tradition in the Dundee area, still using the traditional methods. Of 'the three Js', only journalism still thrives in the city. *The Dandy* and *The Beano* comics, *The Scots Magazine* and the *Dundee Courier*, the comic characters of Desperate Dan, Oor Wullie and the Broons, and many others, all come from the stable of D.C. Thomson & Co. Ltd's publishing empire, which shows no sign of slackening pace. This is the background to the city which became Bamse's home for the ensuing months.

Thorodd re-entered the war at a time when Britain was on its knees. The memory of Dunkirk was still a major scar on the British psyche; the Channel Islands, the only part of the British Isles to be captured by Germany, had been occupied in June 1940; although the RAF's success in the Battle of Britain restored British confidence, hopes were blunted by Hitler's Afrika Corps' successes in North Africa in early 1941. Britain was facing a stark future.

After frustrating months away from the fighting, the Norwegians looked forward eagerly to an exciting change from their past maintenance and training role. They had escaped to Scotland to continue the fight, and now they felt useful again. On 14 March 1941 *Thorodd* joined the 71st Minesweeper Group, which had its headquarters at Dundee and an operative sphere between Dundee and Aberdeen. Her ship's identification, FY 1905, was displayed on her newly painted battleship-grey sides. She joined three other all-Norwegian-crewed minesweeping trawlers *Nordhav II* (FY 1906), *Syrian* (FY 1732) and *Bortind* (number unknown). They were to remain together as a close-knit group for the next three years until *Thorodd* was laid up in 1944. *Nordhav II* did not survive the war; she was torpedoed and sunk in May 1945.

Dundee was an important base for small ships operating in the North Sea, and the Norwegians had a strong presence there in addition to the 71st Minesweeper Group. The Norwegian minesweepers were given berths at the Eastern Wharves at the eastern entrance to Dundee harbour, which soon became known as the Norwegian Wharf. They were joined by two Norwegian submarines, *Ula* and the ill-fated *Uredd*. Across the water at Woodhaven, just upriver from Newport-on-Tay, was stationed a flight of 333 Squadron Royal Norwegian Air Force Catalina flying boats which were engaged in anti-U-boat reconnaissance and attack activities and in carrying out secret missions to Norway. These were all supporting units attached to the Royal Navy's Minesweeper Groups 34 and 104 and sundry armed patrol trawlers, other auxiliary patrol boats and examination service vessels.

Herman Eilertsen arrived in Dundee by train on 5 May 1941, made his way to Earl Grey Dock at the west end of the harbour and reported for duty to HMS *Unicorn*. Built as a 46-gun frigate in 1824, in the glory days of sail, *Unicorn* is the oldest British warship still afloat. She was renamed HMS *Cressy* in 1941 to avoid confusion with the aircraft carrier bearing the same name and played an important role during the war as headquarters of the Senior Naval Officer, Dundee. (She later reverted to her original name in 1959 when the aircraft carrier was scrapped.) Herman arrived at a time when most of the boats were under-crewed, and he was posted to *Bortind* as Oerlikon gunner where he remained until 1943, when he transferred to the submarine *Ula*. His account of the Norwegians in Dundee and his observations about minesweeping are helpful in understanding what happened in those days.

With restricted wharf space, the Norwegian ships were often

'rafted up', with the larger ships *Nordhav II* (which was the command vessel) and *Thorodd* usually lying alongside the quay. When the submarines *Ula* and *Uredd* were in port they rafted up alongside too. The crews on the outer vessels had to scramble across the inner vessels to get to shore and it was a good opportunity for the sailors to mix and get to know each other. They also came in constant contact with Bamse, who was frequently on self-imposed duty on *Thorodd*'s deck or on the quayside. On one occasion he physically restrained a visiting English sailor from making a dangerous jump between two of the ships and dragged the hapless sailor to the proper gangway.

Another graphic example of Bamse's dislike of the effects of alcohol on sailors occurred when a young and inexperienced cadet officer, very much the worse for wear, was struggling to get on board *Nordhav II* and was upended by Bamse, who placed a large paw on his chest and, gazing into his eyes more in sorrow than in anger, pinned him to the deck. The young man could not move until the Officer of the Day requested his release and then gave him a very public tongue-lashing, much to the delight of the other ranks.

Herman saw Bamse accompanying the shore patrol, which was made up of ratings who, under the command of a junior officer or a senior petty officer, went on shore in a policing capacity. Their job was to go round the pubs and night spots to preserve and restore order if any of the sailors were causing trouble, and also to make sure that the men got back to their ships on time. At these times he was the very antithesis of the nanny dog, standing no nonsense from inebriated or belligerent sailors and nipping any likely altercations in the bud.

His principal keeper on board was Albert Andersen, who had been one of the men who had begged to be taken on board as

Thorodd prepared to escape from Tromsø. If bad weather was forecast and Bamse was left on shore, Albert left him in the care of *Nordhav*'s mess steward, who took over responsibility for feeding him and attending to his other domestic needs. It must have always have been at the back of the crew's minds each time she left port without him that *Thorodd* might not return, and arrangements had to be made for the care of their mascot. However, when on board *Thorodd*, as an enlisted member of the crew, Bamse was expected to take his chances along with the others if the ship came under attack.

The clearance of mines was given the highest priority by Allied High Command. In addition to the Norwegian boats that escaped to Britain and, like *Thorodd*, were converted, the Royal Navy requisitioned around 800 British fishing vessels for minesweeping duties, all of which gave magnificent service. For the whole of the war these vessels were deployed day and night to keep the seaways clear and safe, and minesweepers spent more operational hours at sea than any other class of vessel. The motto of the Algerine Association, the membership of which is drawn from the sailors who served on this class of minesweeper, is 'Let there be a way through the water', which speaks volumes about the crucial role the 'little ships' played.

Minesweeping was a hugely important task in World War II, and the courage of those who faced the daily dangers to make the seas safe for their fellow sailors cannot be overemphasised. Despite the reassuring effect of familiar and routine tasks, the sailors must always have had the spectre of the standing naval joke about 'only lasting a fortnight on a minesweeper' at the back of their minds, experiencing bowel-churning moments of fear every time they went to sea. These young men, especially the Norwegians entirely cut off from their homes and families, would have had the need for a compassionate shoulder, an undemanding non-judgemental support when their personal demons were sitting on their backs and they had no one to talk to. It was natural that they should turn to Bamse for consolation, and these would have been the times when he was most responsive to his human companions' emotions.

It wasn't all work and no play in Dundee. The sailors had time off for rest and recreation. Bamse was regularly included in their nights out and booze-ups; he was one of the boys, and was very obviously a favourite with the ladies too. Sailors being sailors, when *Thorodd*'s crew went ashore they hoped to meet the girls, for whom an encounter with a Norwegian sailor was an unusual event, certainly at the start of the war. One of them in the company of a huge St Bernard dog was bound to attract attention, and the sailors quickly realised what a useful social icebreaker Bamse could be when language difficulties hampered conversation. The outcome was that Bamse featured prominently in a number of romances between Dundee girls and the crew members, some of which ended in marriage.

The Grilli family, a second-generation Scottish-Italian family, lived at Church Street, Dundee, where they ran a traditional fish and chip shop, with another branch at the Hilltown. Cesare and Josepina (known to all as Joe and Mary!) had four children. Ernest had joined the Royal Navy and Jean had married and moved to Italy in 1935, leaving Rena (Caesarina) and Louise at home, helping with the family business. The war brought a particular chaos and distress to the lives of the Grillis, as for a time both parents were interned because of their Italian background. Rena, aged 21, was left to look after Louise, and, to add to their problems, the business had to be closed. Dependant so much on each other, the two sisters developed a great closeness. Happily, first Mary and later Joe were released home, and family and business life resumed.

Her strict Catholic parents were not too pleased when Rena met and brought home a tall, handsome Norwegian sailor. He was Einar Andersen, a member of the crew of the minesweeper *Thorodd*, and newly arrived at Dundee. As the youngest daughter of an Italian family, Louise was limited in how much she was allowed to go out, so she had heard about Einar and the ship's dog Bamse from Rena long before she met them. Rena was rather reticent about the Norwegian sailor she had met, but she had plenty to say about the warm, friendly dog who accompanied him about town. Bamse was the ideal antidote to the initial moments of shyness and language difficulties, and Rena hoped to see more of her young man. Joe and Mary were won over by Einar's easy, gentle charm and his love affair with Rena developed rapidly. In light of his previous experience in the merchant marine, Einar expected to be posted to the Arctic convoys, and the couple decided to get married without delay. Theirs was one of the first Norwegian-Scottish weddings to take place in Dundee, and the marriage lasted more than fifty years. They were married at the Norwegian Consulate in the Nethergate by the consul, Mr Pedersen. Just a handful of family and friends were present, and a simple lunch at a hotel followed. The young couple had only a few weeks of married life together before Einar departed for the Murmansk convoys which began in August 1941, and they were not to see each other for a long 18 months. However, the sadness of their parting was softened by the realisation of a new life, for Rena was pregnant.

Before the war, Henry 'A.K.' Johansen was a fisherman from Berlevåg, east of Honningsvåg, in the very far north of Norway. He escaped to Scotland and served on *Thorodd* from 8 January 1941 till 15 January 1944 when he transferred to submarines. After Chief Engineer Anders Larsen, he was the longest-serving sailor on *Thorodd*, and in the course of her duties he visited ports up and down the east coast of Scotland including Rosyth, Dundee, Montrose and Aberdeen. A.K. and his crewmate Albert Andersen, who had a particularly strong bond with Bamse, became close friends and spent many of their shore leaves together. They also began courting two Scottish girls at much the same time.

There are fewer surviving stories about Bamse's time at Port Edgar than about his later years, but it is clear from his behaviour once he settled into life in Dundee that he had spent the previous months usefully interacting with all manner of humans and sharpening his social skills. *Thorodd's* berth at the Eastern Wharves in Dundee was only a short distance from the Lindsay and Lowe munitions factory, which had a largely female workforce. In best naval tradition, Bamse quickly acquired a following of admiring girls among the factory workers. He presented himself at the factory gates at 'piece time', or the meal break, hoping to supplement his rations with leftovers from their sandwiches. Eileen Fagan lived in St David's Lane at the West Port of the harbour, close to the factory, and she was one of the girls who made a fuss of Bamse. In due course the dog engineered a meeting between Eileen and A.K., and soon they were 'walking out' together, often with Bamse at their heels.

Albert, meanwhile, had met Ella, who came from the Fife town of Kirkcaldy. The two started dating, and Bamse was a regular companion. Dancing was a favourite pastime of the Norwegians, and the two couples often went to the Locarno

Ballroom and also frequented the Empress Ballroom, which was near the Royal Arch entrance to the Earl Grey Dock, which later disappeared in 1961 to make way for the Tay Road Bridge. Surprisingly for such a gregarious dog, dancing never featured in Bamse's list of social activities. He does not seem to have gone to the dance halls even as a spectator or canine wallflower. Perhaps it was just as well – he might have regarded dancing as a form of contact sport, and stories of his energetic participation on the dance floor would have matched the tales of his encounters at football matches!

Ella invited Eileen and the two boyfriends to spend a weekend at her home in Kirkcaldy and included Bamse in the party. In the course of one evening, Albert and Ella settled down on the sofa to clear up some points of comparative Norwegian-Scottish etiquette, with Bamse comfortably stretched out in front of the fire. He obviously mistook as cries of distress Ella's squeaks of satisfaction at how readily her and Albert's thoughts harmonised and decided he must intervene. As poor Albert leapt up from the sofa, Bamse rose up on his hind legs and, leaning his whole weight against the hapless lover, pinned him, helpless, to the wall. Once the uproar had subsided and tempers were restored, everyone was greatly amused to see two large paw marks on the wallpaper, about six feet up from the floor.

After a courtship of about a year, A.K. asked his captain's permission to marry Eileen, and the wedding took place on 30 October 1942. Due to wartime shortages, it was a small affair and, for whatever reasons, Bamse does not seem to have been a guest. His intervention during the weekend leave in Kirkcaldy may have drawn Ella and Albert closer, for they too married and after the war set up home in Kirkcaldy.

Time and again the strands of Bamse's story separate and

reconnect. He is the one constant throughout, central to everything, around which all the subplots and their characters develop. A.K. Johansen stayed in the Royal Norwegian Navy until 1949, when he returned to live and work in Dundee. Eileen and A.K.'s son Harry went to sea too, and when he retired as a captain from the Merchant Navy he was appointed harbourmaster at Montrose, where *Thorodd* had spent much of her war, and he still lives in the town where Bamse is buried.

It is remarkable how unreservedly the crew accepted Bamse into their lives, to the extent that they took him away for weekend breaks when it must surely have been easier, and cheaper, to have left him in the safekeeping of the other sailors. Equally fascinating is Bamse's universal affection for all the crew and his readiness to accompany any or all of them on the next adventure. He never showed the usual canine characteristic of needing a single master to whom he would relate.

Bamse was undoubtedly a useful introductory icebreaker between his shipmates and the munitions girls, but Bjørn Hagen remembers that the sailors held an additional attraction. By that stage of the war, tea, like other groceries, was in short supply and rationed. The Norwegians, however, had an apparently unlimited supply. As the factory girls were not allowed on board the ships, gifts of tea from the sailors ensured invitations from the girls to join them on shore. The language barrier rarely posed a problem in the development of the romances, but it could cause difficulties at weddings. As a good English speaker, Bjørn was sometimes asked to support the bridegroom at his wedding and prompt him when he had to say, 'I do.'

Bjørn has several other hilarious observations about some of the lighter moments ashore. The Dundee dance halls could sometimes be rough places – 'snake pits', Bjørn calls them. The dancing often ended in an international brawl between the British, the Poles, the French and the Norwegians. It seemed that no good Saturday night out ended without a proper punch-up. In the morning, though, when wiser counsels prevailed and everyone had forgiven each other, they were all the best of friends again.

Some of the Norwegians got too friendly with married or engaged girls and ended up in bed with them. There were stories of husbands and fiancés returning home so unexpectedly that the sailors had no time to pull on their clothes and were seen running naked through the streets of Dundee back to their ships. 'It was a good thing that the British didn't send their men home on leave with their weapons or there might have been some shootings,' was Bjørn's dry comment. Some fathers warned their daughters against mixing with the Norwegians, telling them that they were 'only after one thing'. Perhaps they were right.

One young lady, keen to prolong the moments of passion with her Norwegian boyfriend, tried to smuggle him into the house through the back door. In the darkness neither of them noticed an uncovered manhole, and the sailor's expectations were painfully thwarted as he stepped into an open sewer instead of a warm embrace!

Olav Nilsen, who had arrived in Scotland as *Syrian*'s navigation officer, transferred to *Thorodd* as second-in-command for a short time while she was based in Dundee. He subsequently rejoined *Syrian* and later commanded her. Jean Christie, daughter of William Christie, and living at Melrose Terrace in Dundee, was a newly qualified nurse on duty at Dundee Royal Infirmary when Olav visited a member of the crew who was ill. Bowled over by the pretty nurse, he made it his business to visit the sailor several times and eventually plucked up the courage to ask Jean for a date. Bamse was not there at the start to smooth the path of love but he must have kept a weather eye on the young couple for they married in 1941. A photograph taken on their wedding day shows how good-looking they both were, and it is easy to understand why they very quickly fell deeply in love. Willie Nilsen, their son, recalls both his parents speaking with great affection about the dog, who they got to know well when they became part of his friendly social circle.

Servicemen in uniform were generally warmly received wherever they went, but, despite the levelling effect of shared wartime privations, Britain still suffered to a degree from pre-war social prejudice and condescension. Whether in or out of uniform, however, the Norwegians were welcomed by their Scottish hosts and they returned this hospitality, albeit on a more emancipated basis. Olav's acceptance by Jean's family was assured after he met her father returning home from work dressed in his dirty work overalls, for he worked at the Caledon shipyard (where the oil support base is now). Without hesitation, Olav took him to the Norwegian officers' mess at the Caird Rest in the Perth Road and introduced him as his future father-in-law. His fellow officers paid no attention to their guest's working dress and made him welcome. Willie recalls that years later his grandfather told him that such a thing could never have happened in a British officers' mess.

Not every friendship between a Dundee lassie and a Norwegian sailor ended in romance. In 1942, Peter Low, then 16, met and became friendly with Bamse. He lived with his parents, his elder sister Ruby, and younger brother Harry in a tiny two-roomed tenement flat at Bellfield Street, in the Hawkhill area of Dundee and about a mile from the docks. In 1940, when Dundee docks were being heavily bombed, Harry and Peter had been evacuated to the relative safety of Montrose, a time of which both boys had happy memories, despite the separation from their parents. Now Peter had left school and was doing odd jobs while waiting to join the Royal Navy, which he did in 1943.

Ruby had joined the Auxiliary Territorial Service (ATS), gaining a measure of freedom from her parents. Shortly after *Thorodd*'s arrival in Dundee, she fell in with the crew and struck up a close friendship, which never grew to be anything more, with Able Seaman Henry Berthling. Although there was no romance, whenever *Thorodd* was in port, Ruby invited Henry home, where he was welcomed as one of the family. On each occasion, Bamse accompanied Henry, and Peter recalled the special bond that was very evident between the two.

During these visits Bamse was unusually docile and engaging and was inseparable from young Harry Low (perhaps because he had flashbacks to the Hafto children and the small house they lived in). The two would play and wrestle for hours and on Harry's command Bamse would rise up on his hind legs to a 'terrifying height'. Too large for the tiny flat, much of the time Bamse was confined to the lobby or the landing on the communal stair, where he lay in noble repose with his paws crossed neatly in front of him. Mrs Low was particularly fond of Bamse and always wanted to know well in advance when his next visit would be so that she could ask the butcher to provide a bone for him.

Ruby kept a wartime diary, now sadly lost, which included many memories of Bamse and his visits to the Low family. She also kept in touch with Henry Berthling, and after she was widowed she planned to visit Norway to see him again. Henry died just four months before she made her visit, but much of her holiday with his widow and family was spent reminiscing about him and Bamse when they had visited the small flat in Dundee. Once again, Bamse's benevolent influence had extended from the grave long after his death.

Margaret Crichton was 34 when war broke out. Her daughter Heather Cochrane recounts that Margaret was tied to a tedious office job and living at home looking after her invalid mother. It seemed that her chances of marrying and having a family were fading. Some years before there had been a love affair and a proposal of marriage from a rubber planter. He was considered a 'good catch', but his family was opposed to Margaret and the engagement was abandoned.

Suddenly Dundee was awash with the excitement of the war effort, and the city became home to thousands of British and Allied sailors, soldiers and airmen. Sometime in 1942 Margaret met Lieutenant Oscar Jensen, who was serving on *Thorodd*. It is probable that they first met at the Royal Hotel at the top end of Union Street or the Queen's Hotel near the railway station, which were both popular gathering places for service people of all nations. Oscar was a large jovial man with an infectious smile. He spoke excellent English, and he was frequently accompanied by the ship's St Bernard dog mascot. Bamse exercised his usual charm and once again played the part of Cupid as he had done so successfully on previous occasions. Secret smiles and fingertips meeting under cover of his thick fur could have been the first steps to passion and romance.

A love affair developed between Margaret and Oscar, but there was a fatal impediment to its fulfilment for Oscar Jensen was already married and had a family in Tromsø. There was no deceit, and Oscar made no attempt to conceal this fact from Margaret or her family. Faced with this reality, the couple determined to remain friends, and a deep friendship endured almost to the end of the war, although both were aware that, in the end, nothing could come of it.

In accordance with the social conventions of the day it was not appropriate for the couple to meet at Margaret's mother's flat, and she would have disapproved in any event. Margaret's married elder sister, Mary Shepherd, lived in a flat in Park Avenue and this became their meeting place. Hampered by convention already, they were hampered further by Bamse, for Oscar often brought the dog with him. His large presence dominated the small flat, and he had to be banished to beneath the dining table, where he lay hidden by its overhanging tablecloth. One morning Mary's teenage son, Gordon, was late for breakfast. After the usual parental lecture, a plate of bacon, eggs and all the trimmings was set before him at the dining table. The beckoning aroma of all the good food proved too much for Bamse, whose head appeared from beneath the tablecloth and the contents of the plate vanished with one sweep of his tongue! Gordon's outrage soon cooled and Bamse was forgiven, but the story entered the Shepherd family folklore, and, even after all these years, Gordon is still teased about the time he was late for breakfast.

Margaret's extended family became very fond of Oscar Jensen, and he of them. Margaret's other sister Betty and her two children Roy and Sheila had endured a miserable time during the Blitz in Southampton, which was particularly hard hit by the bombing because of its importance as a naval port. They desperately wanted a holiday back in Dundee, and in 1943 this became possible. Oscar arranged for them and for Margaret to visit *Thorodd*, and the sisters and the two children were invited on board for lunch. The children, in particular, had a magical time and found a new playmate in ship's dog Bamse, who kept them under close observation to stop them falling overboard. Even in wartime the ship's cook could conjure up treats, and his delicious lunch that day was a welcome relief from the usual monotonous rations.

As the war moved on, *Thorodd* spent less and less time at Dundee, and Oscar and Margaret saw less and less of each other. At some point, maybe when *Thorodd* was taken out of commission in September 1944, Margaret and Oscar stopped seeing each other; the war that had brought them together was coming to an end, and their relationship, which might have held together in other circumstances, had to end with it. If Margaret cherished memories of the times she and Oscar had together, it is easy to believe that she kept a corner in her heart for Bamse too.

Dorothy Brown was only 17 when she and a friend, out on a Sunday stroll, saw some sailors outside the Norwegian forces' club at the Caird Rest. She was puzzled by their accents, until her friend pointed out the Norwegian flashes on their uniforms. This was enough for the sailors to strike up a conversation with them and invite them into the club for tea. Thus it was that Dorothy met Herman Eilertsen, himself only 19, and their romance began.

Dorothy's parents liked Herman from the outset and provided the young sailor with a home from home. Unlike many of their friends who enjoyed drinking and whatever bright lights the blackout permitted in the city centre, the young couple preferred to go dancing at the Palais Ballroom and ice skating. As skating, also, was not one of Bamse's accomplishments, they did not see as much of him as the other couples who frequented the pubs where Bamse could usually be found. Their relationship was interrupted by long periods of separation, especially when Herman was transferred to the submarine *Ula*, and Dorothy preferred not to go out on her own. The relationship did endure, however, and they married in June 1944, just before D-Day. Such was the pressure of Allied plans that Herman had to rush back to his ship the same day. Herman's mother died in the course of the war, and because he could not communicate with his family she died not knowing that she had a daughter-in-law, and even more poignantly not knowing that her two sons, who had escaped to Scotland, survived the war.

Elizabeth Younger became Elizabeth Berg in 1943 when she married Jacob Berg, an able seaman aboard *Nordhav II*. She has clear memories of Bamse, very much the centre of attention, accompanying Norwegian sailors down Murraygate, where Elizabeth worked in a branch of Woolworths. Bamse and his shipmates called into the shop on a number of occasions. Once again Bamse played Cupid and allowed himself to be fussed over by the customers and staff, giving Jacob the opportunity to strike up a conversation with Elizabeth and ask her out. She particularly recalls that shortly before she was married on 27 March the *Scottish Daily Express* published a picture feature and article on Bamse based on his exploits in Dundee. Despite extensive research, this article has not been found, probably because the archives of the Edinburgh edition of the paper were destroyed in a fire. Later accounts by veterans confirmed that there were several newspaper articles featuring Bamse during the war, but unfortunately these have also been impossible to track down. The photographs, in particular, would have provided interesting glimpses of Bamse at the height of his career.

Bamse was a familiar figure around Dundee's docks and the pubs near the harbour area, and like any 'old saut' he had his favourite dens. The Bodega Bar in the Murraygate, the city's business centre, has long gone, but in 1941 it had a busy trade with servicemen. An 1896 photograph of the Murraygate shows a wine shop called Bodega and an adjacent hoarding advertising 'The Bodega Wine Co., purveyors of fine imported wines and Auld Edinburgh Whisky'. Bamse must have been made welcome as 'one of the boys' here, because it became one of his regular haunts. Initially he accompanied his shipmates and got to know the way to the city centre. If he had been left on shore because of bad weather at sea, or his shipmates were drinking in a bar he didn't like, he soon learnt he could get to the Bodega Bar (or the Great Eastern and the Royal Hotel which were also favoured with his custom) and back to the ship without his human escorts.

The months at HMS *Lochinvar* had familiarised him with bus travel, and one day Bamse used his initiative and took the intelligent step of going, unaccompanied, to the regular bus stop on the Broughty Ferry Road, about half a kilometre from the Norwegian Wharf, and waiting for the bus. Again the affinity between dog and man was demonstrated, for the bus driver stopped to let him on. These were the days when buses had conductors, and the conductor allowed him to board. Bamse spontaneously went upstairs because he knew dogs were not allowed to travel in the lower cabin. From his high position, he recognised when he should get off, and the conductor rang the bell for the driver to stop near the Bodega Bar. He doubtless enjoyed a convivial hour with his chums, who bought him a couple of pints and gave him scraps to eat, and after saying his farewells he equally confidently made his way back to *Thorodd*.

Was he as great a favourite of the bus drivers as he was with everyone else he came into contact with, or was he just lucky with the bus staff that day? The word about his journey obviously spread throughout the bus depot because he regularly travelled solo into town, and there are no stories of him being left stranded at the bus stop. However, officialdom stepped in eventually and said that even a dog could not travel on the bus for free. The sailors organised a whip-round and raised the money to buy Bamse'a bus pass, which hung in a pouch round his neck and ensured he had comfortable travel to and from the pub.

The times on shore, the girlfriends, the dancing and drinking were distractions from the daily grind of dangerous minesweeping duties. Sea mines are essentially bombs, terror weapons that are silent, unseen and deadly. A sailor's first knowledge of a mine's presence could be his last mortal thought. It has been estimated that the Axis and Allied powers laid at least 636,000 mines in European and Atlantic waters. Winston Churchill, in his six-volume history of World War II, wrote, 'A significant proportion of our whole war effort had to be devoted to combating the mine. A vast output of material and money was diverted from other tasks, and many men risked their lives night and day in the minesweepers alone.' Mines were a constant threat to naval strategy and tactics, and to merchant shipping, and posed a huge psychological burden on all seamen, not least the crews of the minesweepers themselves.

The task of the minesweepers was to detect and destroy contact mines, magnetic mines and acoustic mines. The ships worked independently, in tandem and in echelon overlapping each other. British minesweepers achieved a record of success in destroying mines, which justified the claim that they were the best minesweepers of any navy in World War II.

The deep draught, designed to counter the weight of heavy fishing gear, of small ships like trawlers and whale-chasers such as *Thorodd* made them ideal for conversion to minesweepers, because the heavy minesweeping gear put a severe drag on the boats operating it. Trawlermen, experienced in pulling long, cumbersome nets through the water, had innate skills that made them natural choices for minesweeping work. Both minesweeping and trawling required patience, and fishermen had the seamanship to maintain a station when minesweepers were working in formation. This seamanship, as well as their experience of working in every sort of sea and weather, must have given *Thorodd*'s sailors more psychological preparation than their comrades in dealing with the fears and anxieties endured by all minesweeper crews.

Contact mines (which were the earliest mines) were spherical in shape and covered in horns projecting from the casing. When a horn was struck by a passing ship, it detonated the mine. The anchored mines, moored to the sea bed, were dealt with by sweeping long cables with cutting devices through the water, deep enough to cut the mine's mooring line. The cutting cable was attached to a torpedo-shaped Oropesa float, or paravane, which carried the cutting line out from the side of the ship, and it was taken down to the required cutting depth by a heavy 'kite' and an 'otter' board. When the cable was cut, the mine surfaced, and it was detonated from the ship by rifle fire or a burst from a Hotchkiss or Lewis machine-gun. The cutting cable was sometimes trailed between two ships, but this could be dangerous if there was an enemy engagement requiring the ships to cut and run. Minesweepers were always vulnerable during air and submarine attacks as their cumbersome gear meant they were slow to take avoiding action. Everyone dreaded drifting contact mines, which posed an even more unpredictable danger than those anchored to the sea floor. The only defence against drifting mines was constant vigilance, and this was especially difficult at night-time.

During sweeping operations it was too dangerous for Bamse to be allowed on the aft deck amongst the sweep gear, hawsers, winding gear and other equipment. However, he gave every appearance of taking an informed interest, and Herman Eilertsen, looking on from *Bortind*, remembered seeing him on the Oerlikon gun table or padding about the forward deck, watching the proceedings intently. The released mines popped to the surface like blowing whales, and Bamse does not seem to have been fazed by the detonations when they were exploded. In an imaginative reversal of its deadly role a defused contact mine has stood outside the Town Buildings in Montrose town centre since the end of the war. Its contents have been replaced by a collecting box for donations to the Shipwrecked Mariners Society.

The magnetic field created by a ship passing over it detonated the magnetic mine. It was countered by trailing from the minesweeper two electrical cables known as long-leg electrodes, in a so-called 'LL sweep'. This created a false magnetic field which set off the mine. The ship itself was protected by a 'degaussing' system which reversed the ship's magnetic field by passing a current through an electric cable round the hull. In the early days, however, the Norwegian minesweepers did not have this technology and magnetic mines remained a continued threat.

Acoustic mines were activated by the sound signature of a ship's propeller. They presented more of a problem, as they needed to be detonated by a noise source before the minesweeper was close enough to be damaged. The most successful solution to the problem was the result of typical British ingenuity. A standard road hammer drill – the Kango hammer – was lowered over the bow in a watertight box. Its vibrations pulsed out ahead of the ship and detonated the mines at a safe distance. The 'Kango sweep' was highly effective and this lifesaving adaptation of their product must have warmed the hearts of the manufacturers, as the machines became standard-issue equipment on all Allied minesweepers. Despite his *sangfroid* under fire, Bamse disliked loud and repetitive noises, and suffered along with the crew during Kango sweep operations. Herman Eilertsen remembers, 'That hammer, going on and on . . . it drove you mad!'

Mines were laid, or 'seeded', by aircraft, U-boats or surface vessels, and it was easy for the Germans to reseed a recently swept area. The frustration of the British crews can be imagined as they crossed and re-crossed familiar waters, keeping the path clear for following ships, which depended on the minesweepers being first on the scene to deal with the hidden killers. The sector between Dundee and Aberdeen was very vulnerable to seeding from the air, as it was within range of German Dornier bombers flying from Sola airbase near Stavanger in Norway. The minesweepers often encountered these planes going about their lethal task, and sometimes the Dorniers came in to harass the ships. *Bortind* was regularly attacked, and responded, as did the other ships when attacked, with long bursts of Oerlikon tracer rounds. Herman Eilertsen was kept busy as *Bortind*'s Oerlikon gunner, but was never able to claim a hit. 'The Germans were too scared to come close,' he explained. 'They headed off home – to my home!'

The 71st Minesweeper Group's dangerous task was compounded by the weariness and boredom of long periods at sea in all weathers. The laying of mines and minesweeping were something of an imprecise science. Minefields were generally laid within specified areas when seeded by ships, but there were no rigid lines along which the mines were dropped, especially from aircraft. Consequently, there was no way of knowing if, or exactly where, mines had been laid, and there was an element of the luck of the draw as to whether the minesweepers could find them. Sometimes a day or two could pass without a single mine being located; on other days they would destroy a dozen.

There were three types of operations. 'Short sweeps' were undertaken to keep the sea lane between Dundee and Aberdeen clear. The ships usually went out for four days and were home for four, in a relentless cycle. If a Norwegian ship was in port for repair, the others worked with their British counterparts from Groups 34 or 104, as they often did when sweeping in formation. A number of Norwegians sailed on the British boats, either attached to the crew, or in British uniform, having joined the Royal Navy. Reciprocally, there were British sailors attached to the Norwegian ships.

An adaptation of the short sweep involved sweeping secret passages through the curtain of defensive mines that lay parallel to Britain's coastline, allowing warships to pass through safely to carry out operations.

'Long sweeps' involved sweeping ahead of the vital Russian convoys as they moved up the east-coast sea lane towards the North Atlantic or Murmansk routes. The little ships moved ahead of the convoys to neutralise the mine threat, sweeping as far as Orkney and Shetland, and they could be away for weeks. Throughout the operation, there was the threat of German bombers from Sola probing the sea space looking for the convoys.

In 1974, Olav Nilsen, accompanied by his son Willie, visited Lunan Bay, a local beauty spot 13 kilometres south of Montrose. Unexpectedly, Olav appeared to be unwell. He was pale and sweating and shaky. Willie, then a medical student at Dundee University was very worried: 'I thought he was having a heart attack. It was very alarming. I sat him down and fortunately he recovered quite quickly. My father could only say, "My God, this is where I could have died." He would not tell me what it was about. He simply would not tell me.'

Herman Eilertsen's account provides the answer. One glorious July day in 1941, the Norwegian flotilla had a very narrow escape. The ships were lying at anchor in Lunan Bay, awaiting a convoy to join them before they began a long sweep. 'It was', says Herman, 'a perfect day in a perfect place.' A Heinkell bomber appeared suddenly over a headland, flying very low and too fast to be identified in time to take defensive action. The plane lifted as it passed over the ships, and the men could see the cigar-like shapes of its bombs as they were released and fell towards them. Rooted in terror, they could do nothing and were deafened by the detonations of violent explosions, then drenched by walls of water. 'When everything had settled down,' recalls Herman, 'it seemed that a miracle had happened. All the bombs had missed the ships, just by feet. There was only minor damage and no one was hurt. We were very, very lucky. We were also very, very shaken.'

Although Bamse's presence lightened the days and months for the ships' crews, much of their time was spent on duty at sea, dealing with the hard reality of their dangerous job. They dreamt of the time when the tide of war would turn in their favour, the enemy would be defeated and they could return home.

They knew that their contribution was valuable. The Bellman's Budget column in the 16 May 1942 issue of the Dundee weekly newspaper the *People's Journal* carried a poem by an anonymous writer 'on board a minesweeper'. It expresses the pride felt about the little ships converted to minesweepers, the fishermen who sailed in them and their contribution to the war effort. It is obviously written about a local northeast-Scottish fishing boat, but the sentiments apply equally to a Norwegian boat like *Thorodd*. 'The following verses', said the columnist, 'paint a graphic picture of the arduous job of the little ships.'

Little Ship

Out you go, little ship,
There's lots of work to do,
You can't lie here in harbour,
If you take the Service view.
You've got to sweep the Channel clear
To let the convoy through,
And be they passing North or South,
It's all the same to you.

Minesweeping is a dreary job,
There's no more to be said;
It isn't like a pleasure cruise,
No warm and cosy bed.
You never know what's coming next,
Or how things lie ahead,
Until you heave your sweep on board
And switch on green and red.

Your craft was built for catching fish,
Your crew were trained that way,
But when the nation needed you
You changed in just a day,
And stowed your trawls and warps ashore,
Perhaps for years to stay,
Then took aboard newfangled gear
To give you new array.

So out you go you little ship,
And let your sweep begin;
We'll be waiting here tomorrow,
We're all your kith and kin.
And when you make your headrope fast,
Be sure you've helped to win
As someone whispers in your ear
The convoy's safely in!

6

Gallant Efforts

Bamse's life experiences by now were varied and numerous, and his character revealed several distinct qualities. There never was any doubt about his physical courage, as the following stories testify. Of genuine heroism is the story recounted by Willie Nilsen about Bamse's intervention which saved his father Olav Nilsen from serious injury, if not death, during the winter of 1941–2.

Olav Nilsen's brush with death occurred at the Victoria Dock, about 1 kilometre upriver from the Norwegian Wharf. It was the dock where regular cargoes of jute from the Indian sub-continent were unloaded, and the old storage sheds that stood there at the time have now been developed as part of Dundee's riverside regeneration plan. Today's Dundonians will still recognise the area, which now has restaurants, retail outlets and offices constructed within the original buildings.

Their father's experience was one of the Nilsen children's favourite bedtime stories and Willie tells it in his own words:

> *Thorodd* was lying at Dundee docks. My father had gone on an evening walk along the quayside, with Bamse following on some distance behind him. A man suddenly appeared and attacked my father. His motive was probably robbery, and he closed in to attack my father with a knife. Bamse saw what was happening

and bounded up the quayside to the rescue. Rising up onto his hind legs, he used his momentum and his great weight to push the man away from my father. Continuing to push him, Bamse steered the staggering man to the edge of the quay, and propelled him into the water below. What later happened with this man is unknown to me.

My mother has informed me that my father's life was in real danger, and that he had been saved without doubt by the quick action of Bamse. My mother often told me this story, at the latest shortly before she died in 1986. I repeated this account in a radio program about Bamse on NRK (Norwegian Broadcasting Corporation) some years ago. This was accepted as fact by our family, and is confirmed by me. It was also confirmed by my older brother Carsten William Nilsen when I last visited him.

Enough remains of the layout of the dock area for it to be still quite possible to envisage the scene as it may have unfolded. In a foreign port, far from home and perhaps rather homesick, the Norwegian officer went for a stroll to a local pub for a glass of whisky or a pint of beer to help forget, for a while at least, the stresses of war and his fears for his family left behind in Norway. The assault must have taken place at dusk when the area was deserted, because not even the most irrational knife-wielding thief would carry out an attack in broad daylight, in full view of several gangs of brawny stevedores. There was, of course, no street lighting as the blackout was in place.

In his uniform, Olav was obviously a member of the armed forces – an ally, a friend – and the last thing on his mind was the thought that he might be the victim of armed robbery. Bales of jute stacked higgledy-piggledy on the quayside provided an ideal hiding place for his assailant. As Olav passed him, the knifeman checked that no one followed on close behind. He did not see the large, placid dog ambling along 100 metres behind, which posed no apparent threat. As he slipped from cover, he drew a long-bladed knife from his belt; he challenged the sailor and demanded money.

Olav's bewilderment can be imagined. He hears a threatening voice in a language that is not his own. What little light there is he sees reflected on the blade of the knife, and he has no weapon of his own. He is alone and nearly half a mile from his ship and his comrades. However, having escaped from his homeland and the Nazis in the most precarious of circumstances after enduring 62 days of war, and fighting once more for his country and that of his hosts too, he is in no mood to be robbed at knifepoint without putting up a fight, and he stands his ground.

Had the thief been aware of Bamse's presence, he would probably have held back and let Olav continue on his way. But raised voices, angry tones and a threatening arm held aloft were more than enough to alert Bamse to his friend's danger and arouse his protective instincts. He responded instantly and bounded up the quayside where the two figures were struggling. Olav was no longer fighting alone. A hundred kilograms of growling beast, rearing up on his hind legs and joining the fracas like a rugby front-row forward, was more than the would-be thief could deal with, and he tried to back away and escape. Bamse would have none of it and was determined to see matters brought to a proper conclusion. It is perhaps attributing too much to him to believe that he consciously pushed the robber into the waters of Victoria Dock in order to halt the fighting – it is more likely that this was just how the scuffling ended – but the sudden, cold immersion quickly took the heat out of the moment's mischief.

The thief was manifestly invading the security cordon that

Bamse had thrown around his friends and, unarguably, the dog very consciously went to his friend's aid. No newspaper report can be found of the fate of the knifeman, but hopefully his experience discouraged him from further wickedness – bad enough at any time, but all the worse in wartime and against an ally! Dundonians are known as friendly folk who are generally kind to incomers, so perhaps it was the hardship of wartime shortages that drove this man to violence.

It is interesting to speculate on Bamse's notoriety had Olav's attacker been a non-swimmer and drowned. If the attacker had died, irrespective of the wartime circumstances and the differing standards of the day, Bamse would have been branded a vicious dog, and would most likely been destroyed. The drowning would have filled a few column inches in the local newspapers and Bamse's story would have been lost as a footnote in history.

On 27 December 1941 the Norwegian Navy took possession of one of the new U-class submarines built at Barrow-in-Furness by Vickers-Armstrong specifically for operations in coastal waters, and named her KNM *Uredd*. She was based at Dundee with sister submarine *Ula*, and under the command of Lieutenant Rolf Q. Røren she carried out seven missions patrolling in Norwegian coastal waters, successfully torpedoing German shipping.

Reidar Pedersen served on *Uredd* between 1942 and 1943. Whenever *Uredd* and *Thorodd* were in port together, the crews had regular contact with each other through their naval duties, and they mixed socially afterwards. Bamse guarding *Thorodd*'s gangplank was a familiar sight, and Reidar clearly remembers often seeing him on shore making his daily round of calls to the other ships. He kept his eye on everyone. Local children had a makeshift football pitch on a piece of waste ground behind the harbour buildings and Bamse included it in his tour of inspection. One morning he thought the teams were ill-matched, so he went back to the ship and rounded up several of the sailors, herding them across to join the game and balance up the teams.

Bamse's sporting nature was never far below the surface. He was a familiar sight at football matches and a vociferous supporter of the Norwegian teams. He played a particularly vocal part in a game in Dundee between Norwegian and Polish sailors, racing up and down the touchline whenever his team looked close to scoring a goal, and barking and yelping whenever they did. He became part of the afternoon's entertainment, and spectators came to games to see Bamse as much as the football. His sport wasn't restricted to the football pitch, though. If the crew had some moments for relaxation when *Thorodd* was at sea they sometimes played a game of informal deck football with a ball made of rolled-up cloths. Bamse observed no rules in these games and regarded himself as a roving player with no allegiance to any side. The rolling deck was scarcely a level playing field and on one occasion the ball went overboard. Without missing a beat, Bamse jumped straight overboard after it. In open sea and with the ship underway, Bamse was in real danger. Realising this, several of the crew jumped into the water too. With some difficulty they got him back on board, waterlogged but triumphant! With stories like these to entertain them, it is little wonder everyone in the area was interested in him and kept up to date with the news of his latest adventures.

One of these adventures is another story of Bamse's selfless

intervention, highlighting his fearlessness of physical risks, and
sea water. An incident around the autumn of 1942 which Reidar
particularly recalled, because he was on the spot at the time,
was a near drowning that Bamse averted at some danger to
himself. Reidar and a member of *Thorodd*'s crew were chatting
on the dockside beside the ships when they were interrupted
by Bamse's barking, which was noisy and prolonged, as though
he was trying to attract the crew's attention. A tremendous
commotion followed by a splash indicated that someone had
fallen overboard. Unlike the Victoria Dock, which is an inner
dock with slack water, the Norwegian Wharf faces directly on
to the river and a person falling in is at the mercy of the tidal
currents and in danger of being swept downriver. No one but
Bamse appeared to have seen what happened, but piecing the
story together afterwards it seems that one of *Thorodd*'s sailors
had come back on board after a particularly heavy drinking
session and made his way across the deck to go below. What
further nonsense he got up to was never ascertained, but he
managed to tumble over the ship's high gunwale and fall into
the river. Only Bamse saw the accident, and barked to raise
the alarm. The splash Reidar heard was Bamse diving into the
River Tay.

The tide was high and the current strong, and because of
his condition the sailor was soon in difficulties. Not being a
member of her crew, Reidar could not board *Thorodd*, and
although he could not see him, he heard the dog still barking
furiously. Bamse kept the sailor afloat, barking all the while,
until *Thorodd*'s crew pulled the two of them to the side of the
ship and hauled them to safety. By the time Bamse was back
on board he was exhausted and in a poor state. His thick coat
was saturated with sea water and had doubled in weight, but he

had managed to keep his head above the surface and had kept his grip on the drunk sailor's clothing, to the risk of his own life. The top rail of the gunwale was about a metre high and probably above Bamse's line of vision, but he cleared it without thought of the consequences, not knowing that he had a drop of about four metres to the water. Even taking into account his thick protective coat, it must have been a painful experience for him to belly flop, as dogs do, into water from that height. 'I am sure that Bamse saved the man's life, by raising the alarm and by keeping him afloat in the water,' asserts Reidar.

There are numerous stories of dogs protecting their masters and their families in moments of danger, but with his extended shipboard family, Bamse assumed an unusually large responsibility well beyond that expected of the average dog. Granted, there were times when his size gave him the confidence to do the right thing, but the wide embrace of his protective and concerned vigilance can hardly be matched in any other dog, in war or at any other time.

In so many ways Bamse touched the lives of those who came in contact with him, and the Norwegian Navy has never allowed the importance of his memory to slide into oblivion. On a wider front, though, it took 40 years for his extraordinary acts of gallantry to receive formal recognition by his own countrymen. It was a further 22 years, in 2006, before a fitting memorial to him was to be erected in his adopted homeland of Scotland. But all that comes towards the end of this book.

Reidar's story has an interesting postscript. He owes his life to an astonishing piece of good luck, but another man paid the price for it. On 31 January 1943 *Uredd* set out on an eighth mission to set six special agents from the Kompani Linge (equivalent to the British SAS) ashore at Bodø and proceed to

Senja to pick up two French submariners who had got separated from the French submarine *Junon*. Space in World War II submarines was limited, so in order to take on the six special agents, six of *Uredd*'s regular crew were left ashore. As Reidar had been married only days before *Uredd* set out on her last voyage, the captain considerately gave him honeymoon leave.

Uredd failed to keep a rendezvous at Lerwick on 19 February and disappeared along with all hands, and without trace. Reidar knew the submarine must have been lost because he had no ship to report to when his leave was up. In line with wartime security measures and the necessity for information to be disseminated only on a need-to-know basis, he did not discover his shipmates' fate until many years later, when, in 1985, KNM *Tana* found her lying in 105 metres of water, southwest of Fugloyver, south of Bodø. She had not sailed far before she had entered an unknown German minefield and was sunk by a mine. The whole crew of 34 sailors and 6 agents were killed. *Uredd* is the only vessel in Norwegian submarine history to have been lost.

Reidar's honeymoon leave saved his life, but, in common with so many others who survived through similar twists of fate, the knowledge that another died in his place is a burden he has carried with him.

Bamse's response to some events makes it easy to believe that there was an aesthetic side to his nature. Although he was a social dog who enjoyed human company, and there were few things he liked better than a good night out, he also had a strong musical streak hidden inside his great frame, and an evening which included music was a special event.

The Norwegian Welfare Committee ran a social and welfare club in a fine imposing building in the Perth Road known as the Caird Rest, where concerts and other entertainment were arranged for the Norwegian troops. The Welfare Committee organised a concert given by the celebrated Norwegian actress and singer Gerd Grieg, who was the wife of officer, war correspondent and writer Nordahl Grieg. He was notable for having been the officer charged with ensuring that the Norwegian gold reserves were safely transferred onto HMS *Devonshire* and taken out of the country when the Norwegian royal family escaped to Britain. He was a staunch opponent of Nazism and died bravely on a bombing raid over Berlin in December 1943.

In the way that coincidences crop up unprompted in the best stories, Nordahl was distantly related to Edvard Grieg, probably Norway's most famous national composer, who was of Scots descent and whose ancestors had farmed Mosstoun of Cairnbulg, north of Aberdeen in the Buchan district of Aberdeenshire. In the Scottish spelling of the name, the letters 'i' and 'e' are transposed and it is spelt more familiarly, to Scots at least, as Greig. No doubt Gerd was aware of this nugget of her husband's family history, which made her trip to Scotland all the more significant.

Gerd was one of Norway's most respected classical singers, but it seems that this had not been well communicated to the crew of *Thorodd* and the other Norwegian servicemen – including Bamse, of course – who crowded into the Caird Rest expecting a sentimental evening of favourite songs from home. Perhaps the organisers had assumed that their famous guest's reputation would have preceded her. Whatever the audience's expectations, the programme was one of classical songs and pieces with which they were unfamiliar. Nevertheless, whether it was their

realisation of Gerd's obvious fame and quality as a singer, or
the audience's innate Norwegian courtesy towards their own
countrywoman, each song was received with polite applause.
Their apparent enthusiasm was unfortunately misinterpreted as
a sign they wanted to hear more, and Gerd and her accompanist
felt encouraged to play an encore.

The audience began to fidget; there were pints of good Scottish
beer waiting to be drunk and girlfriends to be cuddled. Bamse
must have been receiving the cerebral Mayday signals loud and
clear, for he took control of the situation. As the pianist launched
into the first notes of the next song and Gerd's voice filled the
room, Bamse raised his own powerful voice in mournful canine
plainsong. For a few horror-struck moments the performers
and audience were transfixed by this less than tuneful duet,
then the comedy of the situation spilled over and the whole
room dissolved into helpless laughter, rapidly bringing the
concert to an end. The audience departed gratefully to their
favourite watering holes, where no doubt the story grew arms
and legs as it was told and retold, to tuneful accompaniment as
they re-enacted the songs. Bamse's intervention surely got due
recognition, and he was included in the order for several pints
of beer. Hopefully it all appealed to Gerd's sense of humour and
became a favourite dinner-table story that she felt she could tell
against herself.

Bamse's intervention did not save any lives this time, but,
in the way that laughter does, it broke the tension and saved
the situation. There's no knowing whether he was bored after
the evening of classical music, or whether he had picked up
his companions' impatience at the idea of an encore, but he
intuitively chose the right moment to declare his own feelings –
which for all anyone knows may have been a positive response,

and the expression of his appreciation of Gerd's voice and her choice of music.

Fritz Egge, who was with *Thorodd* from July 1943 until August 1944, recounted another entertaining story of a musical night out in Dundee which revealed a hitherto unknown quality in Bamse – a strong sense of chivalry and of what was right and proper.

Vera Lynn was one of Britain's best-loved and most immediately recognisable female singers of World War II, truly a superstar of the time. In recognition of her contribution to wartime morale, entertaining troops at home and overseas, she was appointed Dame Vera Lynn DBE. In 1943 she was at the height of her popularity, universally known as the 'Forces' Sweetheart', and she had just finished making *Rhythm Serenade*, one of three films in which she starred.

Vera was booked to sing at a forces' concert at the National Labour Hall in Dundee. It was a huge attraction and a queue of excited servicemen and Dundonians looking forward to an evening's entertainment with the nation's heartthrob stretched down the street, waiting for the booking office to open. Bamse, who wasn't going to miss a promising night out, had brought along his friend Fritz Egge, and the two were among the crowd. All went well until a group of rowdy Royal Navy sailors, no doubt a little worse for wear after a boozy start to the evening, decided they did not want to wait their turn for tickets and barged their way to the head of the queue.

Perhaps the sailors were more than usually boisterous or the other patrons felt they shouldn't object to the men's behaviour when they were in uniform and possibly back home from active service. In the event nobody challenged them – except the Norwegian sailor, who took exception to his fellow sailors' selfishness and urged his shipmate to sort them out. Bamse padded quietly up behind the noisy revellers and applied his usual effective and unconventional method of behaviour control, subjecting the nearest queue-jumper to a lesson in good manners he was scarcely expecting. Rising up on his hind legs, he placed his paws on his unsuspecting victim's shoulders. The sailor was terrified and buckled under Bamse's weight, collapsing on the pavement, pinned down by the dog. His startled companions took fright and backed away, retreating to the end of the queue and muttering dark words about 'bloody Norwegians and their bloody dogs'. Bamse's towering six-foot presence restored an immediate sense of order to the evening and doubtless everyone, including the boozy sailors once they had sobered up, enjoyed listening to their favourite singer.

Bamse was good at interpreting the world he lived in and he recognised that the sailors were behaving out of turn. He could identify which human behaviour was acceptable and which was not, and he intuitively knew how to take control of the situation. He did not fear for his own safety and had the confidence to restore harmony to such situations. His chivalry on this occasion was an almost human response to intimidation. The friendship between Fritz and Bamse remained very strong and Fritz never forgot his canine companion. He regularly visited Bamse's grave in Montrose until his own death in 2000.

The addition of extra accommodation when she was converted to a minesweeper had had an unforeseen affect on *Thorodd*'s seaworthiness. She had been converted to do a job she had not been designed for and the conversion affected her centre of gravity, making her unstable. Naval records show that she was taken out of service for eight months from 8 August 1941 till 28 April 1942 for the fitting of ballast. It was a long time to be out of action, and there may have been difficulties in determining the most effective ballast for her, the choice being generally between solids and liquids. Informed opinion suggests it was likely to have been solids, which could range between lead ingots, bricks, stone, sand or concrete. The addition of ballast generally means sacrificing another feature on the boat, in part or in whole; in *Thorodd*'s case it most probably meant removing some of the fuel tanks, reducing her fuel-carrying capacity and consequently her range at sea.

During the winter of 1941-2, *Thorodd* had shipyard work carried out at Arbuthnott's shipyard at Montrose, 50 kilometres to the north. Willie Nilsen tells of his father Olav giving his mother Jean a joyride on *Thorodd* from Dundee to Montrose, which probably happened after they were married in 1941. To think that a wife would be carried on a naval vessel in peacetime, let alone at the height of wartime activities and in such a dangerous stretch of sea, is inconceivable in the Royal Navy. So, too, is the presence of such a large dog on board. But the Norwegian Navy seems to have taken such irregularities in its stride, and in the wider context of the problems the Norwegians had left behind them, and the daily dangers they faced at sea, wives and dogs on board ship were of small consequence.

Thorodd is known to have been the only ship in the 71st Minesweeper Group to have spent time at Montrose. It is likely that this was due initially to these ballasting problems, as *Thorodd* is first reported as being in the town for the shipyard work at Arbuthnott's during the 1941-2 refit. Recurrent stability problems and routine maintenance needs brought the ship back to Montrose repeatedly during the rest of the war, with her spending increasingly more time there and less in Dundee. Her restricted fuel range meant that her operations were more efficiently conducted from Montrose, which lay in the centre of the minesweeping sector. The town effectively became *Thorodd*'s new base, and her crew, including Bamse, became fully integrated into the life of Montrose and its townsfolk.

Ship's dog Bamse, official Royal Norwegian Navy picture

Commander Erling Hafto, owner of Bamse and captain of KNM *Thorodd*

Above. Kjersti, Gunnar Helge and Torbjør Hafto at Honningsvåg, 1935.
© Vigdis Hafto

Left. Vigdis Hafto at Honningsvåg, 1937.
© Vigdis Hafto

Honningsvåg before the war

KNM *Thorodd*

Above left. Man of war: Bamse in his helmet

Above right. Bamse with Chief Engineer Anders Christian Larsen: the two longest serving crew members on *Thorodd*

Left. Lt Olav Nilsen and Jean Christie on their wedding day

Above left. Deck pet – Bamse with 'A.K.' Johansen (L) and Chief Larsen (R)

Above right. Bamse with crew members (unidentified)

Right. Bath time

Menagerie. Bamse, Nikken and Katt with (R to L) 'A.K.' Johansen, Albert Andersen and three un-named admirers.

Burial in the dunes at Montrose. *D.C. Thomson & Co*

Honningsvåg razed. Hitler's signature – Honningsvåg 1945 – only the church survived. *Nordkappmuseet*

Hammerfest razed. At least there were fish in the sea

Above. Gunnar-Helge and Vigdis Hafto 1949, the time of their pilgrimage to Bamse's grave

Left. Norges Hundeorden, 1984: Vigdis Hafto with Gerd Darner

The Bamse Project Logo designed by Michelle Goring.
© Montrose Heritage Trust

Bamse's grave – restored 2006

Gold medal day at The House of Dun, Montrose. Vigdis Hafto with the gold medal,
Brit the St Bernard and Freddie Bircher, Chairman of PDSA.
Reproduced courtesy of PDSA.

The Doctor and the Lady in the Hat. Andrew Orr and Henny King just before the
unveiling. *Paul Reid.*

HRH Prince Andrew, The Duke of York, shares memories with Vigdis Hafto.
Paul Reid

HRH Prince Andrew, The Duke of York, unveils the statue of Bamse, 17 October
2006. *Paul Reid*

7

Bamse's Manor

The Royal Burgh of Montrose occupies an almost unique geographical position on a spur of land with water on three sides, which separates the tidal Montrose Basin, now an internationally important nature reserve, from the North Sea. The town is one of Scotland's oldest royal burghs and received its Royal Charter, which granted important trading rights to its merchants, from King David I in 1140. It has a fine natural harbour, which in the past was restricted in the size of vessel it could accept, owing to a large sandbank on the north side of the harbour entrance called the Annat Bank. Described as 'that fatal sand', for centuries the Annat was the graveyard of vessels driven onto it by adverse sea conditions or whose masters paid the sandbank too little respect and suffered the consequences.

The port gained prominence originally from local coastal trade, but in the 17th century contacts were developed with the Hanseatic and Baltic countries, and the range of goods imported and exported through Montrose contributed significantly to the economy of the town – so much so that the fledgling Bank of Scotland opened one of its earliest branches in the town in 1696, one year after it was constituted by an act of the original Scottish Parliament. Trading links with Norway were established and by the end of the 17th century there was a busy trade in grain and textiles sailing from Montrose to Norway, with the 'hamebringing' of timber by the returning ships. By World War II, cultural and family ties had drawn Scotland and Norway closer together and created between the two countries a sense of kinship that would prove significant.

In the 1970s the River South Esk's south outflow channel from the Montrose Basin, known as the Inch Burn, was reclaimed to provide land for the construction of an oil support base on Rossie Island. Montrose Port Authority acquired a south quay on the other side of the river, opposite the original harbour, and the port authority now encompasses a considerably larger area than it did in the wartime 1940s. At that time, it comprised only a north quay on the Montrose side of the River South Esk, which stretched downriver about 400 metres to the Wet Dock and Arbuthnott's shipbuilding yard. Its importance as a port had by this time declined considerably from the heady days of sailing ships when Montrose was second in importance only to Edinburgh's port of Leith. Because of its deepwater approaches and berthage, Dundee could accommodate much larger cargo ships and warships than Montrose. The contrast between the two ports was marked, and when *Thorodd* arrived in Montrose she was one of the largest ships in port. However, the war revived Montrose's historic importance, said to date back as early as Roman times, as an anchorage for naval vessels on Scotland's northeast coast.

Its size apart, other differences with Dundee would have been apparent to *Thorodd*'s crew when they first saw Montrose. Its harbour area was very much more integrated with the town (as it still is) than that of Dundee, where port and town are separated by the railway and a busy main thoroughfare. A choice of pubs was scarcely more than a crisp 7-iron golf shot from *Thorodd*'s regular berth at Montrose's Wet Dock, so the crew's journey back to the ship after a regular night's drinking was a lot more direct and easier than the longer route from their nearest hostelry in Dundee would have been!

Bamse had led a charmed and spoilt life on shore at Dundee, but Montrose's social amenities and entertainment were much closer to hand, and with his outgoing and gregarious nature he took all the changes in his stride and rapidly adapted to Montrose's comparative informality. Bamse's 'manor' in Montrose mostly comprised streets with butchers, bakers and grocers, all within a kilometre's radius of the harbour. He soon ensured he was welcome at all of them and could count on being offered scraps of meat, broken pies and biscuits, and the occasional pint of beer along the way, to sustain him during his busy daily programme. It took a lot of food to satisfy the appetite of the biggest dog in the Allied Forces and because of wartime rationing he was almost permanently hungry. The stories telling that he cheerfully gulped down raw fish thrown onto *Thorodd*'s deck by passing fishermen are confirmed by senior Montrosians who were children when they saw him do it.

He might have been offered salmon as a treat on several occasions. The minesweepers generally met northbound convoys at Lunan Bay, and if the convoys were delayed the crews 'swung the lead' while they waited and looked for something to pass the time. Bjørn Hagen was a keen fisherman, and he learned that Lunan Bay was on the annual migratory route of salmon swimming to their mother rivers to spawn, or lay the eggs that would provide the next generation of the king of fish. In the spring the waters just offshore teemed with the salmon run heading for rivers like the South and North Esk and the famous Aberdeenshire Dee and Don. Bjørn couldn't resist the temptation to fish for a salmon, even though he knew it was illegal to catch one with rod and line at sea. (Salmon might only be caught by fixed nets in the sea.) His luck held and he hooked a large salmon, which he had great difficulty in playing. His mates took advantage of the situation, telling him what a criminal he was, and offering 'helpful' suggestions – 'Why don't you jump overboard and swim to the shore and land your fish there!' Bjørn did land his illegal fish and it would be fitting to think that Bamse shared in the feast.

'Shipshape and Bristol fashion' was a standard Bamse clearly advocated. He liked everything spick and span and in its place. One day, taking advantage of time in port, the ship's cook had pulled the large cooking kettles out of the galley onto the deck and was hard at work cleaning them. Ever keen to lend a hand, or a paw in this case, all that could be seen of Bamse was his wagging rear end as he got 'stuck in', almost literally, inside one of the kettles, noisily licking it clean with his great pink tongue. By the time he finished he had succeeded in coating all his fur with old grease and cooking fat redolent of several recent tasty meals he had shared with his shipmates. They were horrified by the state he had got himself into, and the captain insisted that he must be taken to the local vet's surgery to be professionally washed and cleaned. A fee of £1 was agreed upon and the sailors were told to return in an hour. When they did, Mr Rice, the very exasperated vet, demanded £2 because of Bamse's determined opposition to being washed by strangers and the uproar he had caused before he could eventually be hosed down and shampooed. He made it clear that the next time Bamse got so filthy the crew would have to deal with him themselves.

For its size, Montrose harbour was a busy place during the war. Near its west end at the Lazy Hole, beside the old fish pier, were stationed two fast RAF rescue craft. These regularly dashed down the river at high speed whenever there was a call-out to recover air crew who had been shot down or had ditched in the North Sea. Perhaps it says something about inter-service rivalry that the Fleet Air Arm had their own rescue boats moored at Montrose too! Lying close by were two Royal Navy MFV (motor fishing vessel) patrol boats, which had Montrose as their home port. Bob Milne, who lived at the bottom end of Castle Street, remembers them as fast, glamorous boats, which always drew admiration from all the young boys who had almost unfettered access to the dock area as a playground until the authorities 'put up some ropes – to dodge under!'

In addition to naval vessels, the port was busy with commercial and fishing traffic, including several Norwegian fishing boats. The Admiralty patrol boat *The Duthies* was sunk and three of her crew injured during a big air raid – big by Montrose standards – on 25 October 1940 when the railway bridge, the Chivers & Son jam and jelly factory, which fronted onto the harbour, and the Montrose air station were hit. The Norwegian fishing boat *Janet* was also hit and sunk at her moorings, but luckily no one was on board. She was raised and repaired and returned to fishing, but the aerodrome was not so fortunate. The airfield was the Germans' main target, and the four bombs they dropped on it destroyed or damaged 17 aircraft and killed or injured 26 RAF personnel. The officers' mess was completely destroyed by fire, but the squadron's safe, which contained the entire station's pay, appeared to have escaped unscathed. However, once it had cooled, the safe was opened, and, as soon as the cool air hit the hot paper, the notes crumbled to dust.

William Coull from Ferryden recorded his own boyhood memories of that attack in his book *Tales from the Southesk River*

Bank. Narrating the story from the perspective of himself as a young schoolboy in the company of his friend David, he wrote:

> We were 'up the Den' – Usan road – when we heard the planes. The sound of aeroplane engines was no stranger to our ears. We had lived with it for years and hardly needed to look up to recognise Miles Masters, Miles Magisters, Oxfords, Blenheims, Avro Ansons, Spitfires and Hurricanes. They had been our constant companions for years; taking off, circling the town and landing day and night if the weather was suitable. Hundreds of men had been trained to fly at RAF Montrose.
>
> Tonight was to be something different.
>
> The sound that was coming from the southeast was a heavy drone. It was obviously from a number of large planes. We were between Inchbrayock House and Ferryden farm and freewheeled down the brae. Within a few seconds we were at the foot o' the Den.
>
> It was a lovely October evening. The sun had sunk behind low clouds to the west; clouds that were displaying every shade of red and yellow.
>
> With a roar of engines three planes arrived flying just higher than Ferryden church steeple.
>
> Suddenly seven or eight black objects fell from the leading plane. We needed nobody to tell us they were bombs. We knew what to do; get indoors or up a close and if this was not possible, lie down. We lay down. Suddenly our ears were assailed by the loudest noise we had ever heard. It was deafening and frightening.
>
> When we stood up the planes were over the town. Coloured lights flew through the air in all directions. We knew they were tracer bullets and knew they could kill. A steamboat coming up the river was giving and receiving much of the fire.
>
> After a short lull the sound of big explosions was again heard. 'That's the aerodrome getting it,' said David.
>
> At this my father came along wearing his ARP helmet. He told

me to go home. My mother was in the house alone and terrified.

My father went along to the west end of Ferryden to see if he could help. There was little damage other than shrapnel from the first bomb, which had landed on the beach. One piece had gone right through the door of the village policeman.

The Montrose lifeboat, RNLI *Good Hope*, had to deal with many wartime incidents. At 0100 hours on 6 June 1941 the lifeboat station received a report from the coastguard that a convoy had been attacked by enemy planes some 20 kilometres off Montrose. The lifeboat was launched and reached ss *Queensbury* of London, which had been bombed and was ablaze from stem to stern. Coxswain of the lifeboat was Andrew Mearns, who, in his capacity as harbour pilot, piloted *Thorodd* in and out of Montrose, and consequently knew the ship, and Bamse, well. *Good Hope* rescued twelve men, one of whom sadly subsequently died of his injuries. The *Queensbury* was carrying a cargo of lard which had turned her into a blazing torch when she went on fire. For years after the end of the war, lumps of lard from the wreck were periodically washed up on local beaches.

Lifeboats were launched whatever the weather, without protective armament, on missions purely of mercy. Comparably, the lifeboat crews risked their lives as much as any of the other marine rescue services, and were as courageous. As well as being lifeboat coxswain and harbour pilot, Andrew Mearns was a full-time fisherman with the byname of Codling. The use of bynames developed in northeast Scotland as a means of identifying individuals within the isolated fishing communities where there were only a few family surnames. Codling named his boat *Boy Andrew* after his son Andrew Junior, who was born the same year the boat was launched, and who, in his turn, later played a part in sustaining Bamse's memory.

Montrose's lifeboat station is notable for being the oldest continuously manned station in the service, dating back to 1800, 24 years before the foundation of the RNLI. As a historical aside, there is a report that in November 1916 during an earlier war the Montrose lifeboat crew were honoured by the Norwegian government for their rescue of the schooner *Heidstad* and her seven crew.

Seven years old when war broke out, Alex Henderson lived with his parents in Ferryden, a historic fishing community strung along the south bank of the River South Esk, on the opposite side of the water from Montrose harbour. The family home in Beacon Terrace had elevated views east to Scurdie Ness lighthouse at the river mouth, west towards Montrose Basin and the Grampian Hills beyond, and north to the town itself. For Alex and his friends at Ferryden School, the wartime activity on the other side of the river was their major distraction. *Thorodd* became an increasingly regular visitor to Montrose, and Alex's possibly most enduring memory of those days is of *Thorodd* sailing in and out of port with Bamse standing at her bow on the Oerlikon gun platform. He cannot remember a single occasion, out of dozens, when Bamse was not at his self-appointed post, and more often than not he was wearing his sailor's hat.

Doug Anderson has lived all his life in Montrose and was a teenager during the war years. The family home was in Capper's Wynd (now demolished) which was a small lane connecting Wharf Street with Seagate, obviously placing it close to the harbour area. The Seagate leads onto Castle Street, and Donald Cooper, who is likewise a lifetime resident of Montrose, was brought up here, at number 75, in the 1940s. Both men have similar memories of Bamse's activities on shore.

Castle Street in those days was full of small independent shops of which only one, bakers W.J. Johnston, still survives. The shops predominantly served the south end of the town, which was known as the navy end (as opposed to the north end of the town which was referred to as the RAF end because of its proximity to the aerodrome). Despite wartime shortages, Castle Street still had three flourishing butcher shops, Willie Ewen, Jas White and Watty Donald, and four bakers, Johnston, Robertson, 'Pie' MacLean and Cameron. There were four grocers, Salmond, MacFarlane, Dunbar and Todd, and, lastly, Balneaves' and Rocco's fish and chip shops, purveyors of the mainstay of the Scottish diet.

The attractions of Castle Street were a magnet to Bamse, more so because they were on his doorstep. *Thorodd* had hardly tied up at her usual berth after minesweeping duties when Bamse padded off down the gangplank heading for one of his favourite haunts in what, in his mind, he probably perceived as 'Grub Street'. He usually timed his calls for the morning when the shops were full of newly baked bread and the day's deliveries of fresh food, and he moved up the street from shop to shop, unobtrusively reminding the shopkeepers of his presence and appetite. St Bernards are naturally solemn-looking dogs and there are many memories of Bamse appearing at shop doorways with a look of haggard starvation on his expressive face. Even in those days of shortages, his heartrending expression broke down all barriers and he rarely left a shop without some scraps or other to sustain him as far as the next one.

He was the most of appreciative of callers and never made a nuisance of himself, apart from one memorable occasion when he helped himself to a string of sausages placed too tantalisingly close to the open doorway of Ewen's butcher shop for any self-respecting dog to resist. With wartime rationing in place every sausage counted, and Bamse's theft caused quite a stir. He was forgiven when his defenders explained he had suffered a momentary episode of canine disorientation and Mr Ewen made sure he did not make the same mistake again.

Jessie Moig (now Mrs Paton) was born in 1937, the same year as Bamse. She grew up at 56 Castle Street, above Ewen's butcher shop. Her abiding memory of Bamse was his sheer size. He was the largest dog she and her friends, aged six and seven at the time, had ever seen, and he was a great favourite with all the local residents who described him as 'a big couthy [gentle] beast'. He made his presence known as soon as his ship tied up: 'You knew when *Thorodd* was in port,' she recalled, 'he looked as if he owned the place' – confirmation, if it was needed, of his self-assurance.

In those days, one of Montrose's old merchant houses, Balmain House, stood at the top end of Castle Street, at its junction with Balmain Street. Next door was Ramsay House, another merchant house built in the glory days of the town's commercial expansion in the 18th century. Both houses were used as wartime billets and were home to servicemen of several nations. As part of their contribution to the war effort, the owners had removed the handsome iron railings on the stone walls around the houses. Thousands of similar railings all over Scotland were removed for the same purpose, and it is sad that the authorities failed to point out that because they were cast iron, and not steel, they were quite unsuitable for melting down and recycling into aeroplanes and ships and tanks. Without their railings, the low garden walls offered grandstand seating for the children, and it was a favourite haunt for them to congregate and watch the world go by.

On the other side of the street was Mrs Rocco's chip shop, arguably the best in town, and its popularity was confirmed each evening by the hungry queue stretching out along the pavement. The children on the wall watched the customers coming and going, hoping for a hand-out of a few freshly fried chips. The Norwegian sailors were regular customers, usually accompanied by Bamse, who patiently waited his turn in the queue. He loved fish and chips and could always expect to share in his shipmates' fish suppers. As often as not, he ambled across to say hello to the children and allowed them to climb onto his back, digging their little hands deep into his thick fur so he could give them rides up and down the street. The excitement of these childhood adventures is still fresh in Jessie's memory.

Jessie attended Southesk School (still known locally as the 'Soothie'), which, as its name suggests, is close to the river and the harbour. Next door are the factory buildings occupied during the war by Chivers & Son, who built their factory in Montrose because of the availability of high-quality soft fruit, especially raspberries, for which the northeast of Scotland is famous. Seasonal smells of jam- and jelly-making wafted over the playground tantalisingly, teasing the Southesk pupils who were starved of sweet things because of wartime rationing. Jessie remembers Bamse regularly calling at the school to visit the children at breaktime, but the head teacher forbade bareback rides in the playground. Bamse became a great favourite with the children and when they heard of his death they felt as though they had lost a member of their own family.

Having young children round him again must have revived the good times and happy memories of life with the Hafto children tucked away in Bamse's subconscious. He was a generous-hearted dog anyway, and being nanny dog to a new extended family of Scottish youngsters obviously gave him pleasure as he spontaneously sought out their company. The local east-coast dialect may have been unfamiliar to him at first, but children the world over don't let a language barrier get in their way. Jessie and her friends spoiled Bamse with titbits of food, which was the quickest way to gain the big dog's affection.

Ferry Street is the main thoroughfare linking Montrose High Street with the harbour, so was in the heart of the navy end of town during the war. It too held attractions for Bamse. The Anchor Bar is the first pub the sailors coming off duty could have visited, while several hundred metres nearer the town centre is the Caledonian Bar, owned for two generations by the Christieson family and known locally as Catzers. Bamse was a regular at both establishments, and he had a favourite vantage point on the corner of Ferry Street and Caledonia Street from where he had a clear view of both the Anchor and the Caledonia bars and could keep a weather eye open for sailors going in or coming out of either.

Next door to Catzers, at number 18, is Thomas Frost & Sons, another family bakery and confectionery business which, like W.J. Johnston in Castle Street, was on Bamse's daily beat for extra rations (and, like Johnston's, is still very much in business today). As a teenager during the war, Tom Frost was expected to work all available hours in the bakery, which included making deliveries with the horse-drawn van. *Thorodd* shared her time between duties at sea and periods tied up in Montrose and Dundee, often for a week or two at a time. The staff at Frosties' knew whenever she was in Montrose, for Bamse would appear in the small garden at the rear of the shop.

His technique was subtle and astute. He sat silently at the garden gate, neither barking nor whining to draw attention to himself, and making no attempt to enter the bakery. Still as a statue he waited for someone to glance in his direction, at which point he would tilt his head slightly to one side and transfix them with the appeal of his doleful, hungry eyes. It rarely failed to work, and he was soon rewarded with broken pies, pastries and other scraps. He was not a fussy eater, but he ate neatly and straight from the hand. He never begged for more, and when he was finished he turned and sauntered off. He is remembered by the bakery as an extremely well-mannered dog, and he never took advantage of the staff's kindness by trying to enter the shop. It is hard to dismiss the thought that he had worked out for himself that it was easier to obtain small snacks from lots of shops than a feast from a few.

Catzers was popular with his shipmates and Bamse was often seen stretched out on the pavement while the crew drank inside. From time to time, one of them appeared with a pint of beer in a bowl and set it down beside him. Tom Frost clearly recalls seeing Bamse at closing time shepherding crew members, often the worse for drink, back to *Thorodd*.

Moira Ross's story is another that has entered family tradition. Aged only two at the time, she has no personal recollection of what happened, but the story itself and Bamse's benign influence remain fresh in her memory. Mrs Anne Ross was as proud as any mother of her daughter Moira and regularly pushed her for long walks in the fresh air in an expensively upholstered Silver Cross pram that was the envy of the neighbourhood. The family lived in Mill Lane, a narrow lane running parallel to, and terminating at, the harbour end of Ferry Street, behind the Anchor Bar.

Anne, with daughter in her pram as usual, was returning home from Frosties' with some cakes for tea. As she passed the Caledonian Bar and turned the corner into Commerce Street, she was totally unprepared for the appearance of an immense dog from the side door of the bar. The creature put his head into the pram, and, to get a better look at what was inside, rose up and rested his paws on the rim, tilting the pram alarmingly. Anne's screams of terror brought two sailors rushing from the bar who calmed the frightened mother, and, so the story goes, Bamse was so taken aback at the amount of excitement his enquiring interest had aroused that he had to sit down for a few moments to regain his own composure. Once the panic had passed and introductions were made, Anne produced a bun for Bamse from her shopping basket, and the sailors and their dog accompanied her and Moira the short distance home.

Kindness brings its own reward, and Anne's understanding response led to Bamse turning up on her doorstep on his own several days later, seeking congenial company – and another Frosties' bun no doubt – while his shipmates were drinking nearby in the Anchor Bar. Unperturbed this time, Anne Ross let him in, and in a short time they became, and remained, great friends. He was a regular visitor whenever *Thorodd* was in port and sometimes joined Anne and Moira on their daily walks.

As a piece of the small change of Montrose life during World War II, the division of Montrose into the RAF end and the navy end produced a state of affairs much more associated with present times. With so many of the fathers away in service and youngsters not subjected to male parental control, numerous street gangs formed. These fought bitterly amongst themselves, but they would not cross the invisible (and now long-forgotten!) boundary separating north and south to fight with the gangs of a different loyalty. It is interesting how few Montrosians who lived in the northern divide of the town have any knowledge or recollection at all of Bamse. It seems he stayed firmly within the bounds of the navy end, apart from an introductory tour shortly after he arrived in Montrose, up the High Street and along Murray Street.

The Harper family lived in Murray Lane and young Jack was just 14 at the outbreak of war. Restless with all the wartime excitement, he decided to leave school and get a job. He was lucky to find an apprenticeship as a cobbler with Robert Ogston on Murray Street, which was reached by a connecting close, or alley, so he had only a short distance to walk from home to work. One summer evening in 1942, he was entrusted with shutting up the shop at close of business. As he locked up, a large crowd, 50 or 60 strong, was blocking the roadway and holding up traffic at the Port, where Montrose's wide High Street narrows at the old town gate, or 'port', and becomes Murray Street.

'It's the Norwegians,' someone told him helpfully, and, sure enough, he could make out about eight tough-looking sailors. However, they were not the centre of attention; rather it was an animal which, from the back of the crowd, seemed to be a donkey! Ever more curious, Jack wormed his way through to the front and saw that the animal was a very large dog, wearing a sailor's hat and collar and clearly enjoying the attention from the crowd. The cheerful Norwegians were explaining in Norwegian, which made communication difficult, that their companion was Bamse, the famous ship's dog, and they were introducing him around the town. Jack followed the procession as far as his home but cannot recollect seeing Bamse at the RAF end of Montrose again. He was one of a group of elderly guests presented to HRH The Duke of York when he unveiled the statue of Bamse on

17 October 2006. He told the duke that the statue was exactly like the dog he remembered all those years ago.

On the wider world stage, great things were happening which justified the uncertainty and hazards of life on a minesweeper. In October 1942, Lieutenant General Bernard Montgomery led the British Eighth Army and the Allies to victory at the Second Battle of El Alamein, putting an end to German and Axis hopes of victory in the North Africa Campaign. In early 1943, Norwegian resistance commandos destroyed the heavy water plant in the mountains of Telemark, in south Norway, denying Germany the most critical component in the production of the atom bomb. It was one of the most difficult assignments of World War II, and if they had failed the outcome of the war for the Allies would likely have been disastrous.

In operational terms, life on board *Thorodd* was no less dangerous than before and while the end of the war was not yet in sight, the tide was turning against the German aggressors.

8

Dog Days

Einar Andersen, whose experience of the Arctic waters had been responsible for his transfer to the Arctic convoys, was posted back to *Thorodd* in the summer of 1943 because the convoys stopped between March and November of that year.

British and American convoys had provided a lifeline for the beleaguered Russian allies, delivering aircraft, tanks and other vital supplies, and running the gauntlet round the northern coast of German-occupied Norway. They had been under constant threat of attack from German submarines and surface ships, as well as from the air. The vicious winter gales and, the closer they got to the Arctic Circle, the build-up, on the upper parts of the ships, of ice which had to be constantly chipped away to avoid the vessels becoming top-heavy and capsizing, were other ever-present fears. The cry of 'Man overboard!' was simply ignored because it was too dangerous for a ship to turn back for fear of torpedo attack and the loss of even greater life. In any event, the life expectancy of a sailor falling into the near-freezing waters could be counted only in minutes. Life for the convoy crews was as grim and hellish as anything experienced by sailors elsewhere, and ships and crews were pushed almost to the limit of their endurance. Einar was one of the lucky ones – more than 3,000

Merchant Navy and Royal Navy sailors did not return from the runs to Murmansk and Archangel.

Einar's welcome return to *Thorodd* reunited him with old friends, particularly Bamse, and with his wife Rena, whom he had not seen for a year and a half. She had been pregnant when they had said farewell to each other, but sadly the baby had died aged only seven months, when Einar was far from home. Einar never met his child, and so the happiness of seeing Rena again was tempered with sadness.

There was only a skeleton crew on board *Thorodd* when he returned, because it seems the ship was tied up in Montrose for repairs and not likely to go to sea for several weeks. There were, therefore, berths available on board, and by a remarkable and liberal relaxation of the rules, Rena was allowed to join her husband on board. Perhaps this was out of sympathy for their long separation but it was to prove to be their second honeymoon and an idyllic interlude for them in the turmoil of the war.

Their resumed married bliss was disrupted by Rena's younger sister Louise, now 15 years old and off school for the summer holidays. Holidays usually meant long hours working in the family business, but Louise missed her older sister dreadfully and begged her parents to let her travel on her own to Montrose to visit Rena on *Thorodd*. This was quite an adventure as Louise had not been allowed away from home on her own before. It was not possible to contact Rena on the ship and alert her about the intended visit, which came as a surprise. Arriving by train from Dundee, Louise walked down Ferry Street towards the docks, past the Customs House and there, the only ship flying the Norwegian flag, was *Thorodd* – she knew she had arrived.

Apprehensively, she approached the gangway, which was

guarded by a tough-looking sailor with a rifle and an even more ferocious giant dog – Bamse. 'Excuse me, sir,' she said. 'I'm looking for Einar Andersen.'

'What are you wanting with a married man?' demanded the sailor.

'He's my big brother . . . in law!' blurted out Louise.

The surprised couple welcomed their unexpected visitor, and as she stepped up the gangway Einar introduced Louise to Bamse, identifying her as a friend who was allowed on board (for Bamse permitted nobody on board whom he did not recognise). The crew made a great fuss of her arrival and food quickly appeared in the saloon. The visit turned out to be hugely exciting, and Louise found she was enjoying the best day of her life. 'I don't want to go home – can't I stay here with you?' she implored her sister. The Norwegian authorities' tolerant attitude, however, did not stretch so far as to allow a teenage girl to stay on board *Thorodd* overnight, so the sisters went to find a public telephone and Rena phoned her parents to ask their agreement to another plan.

Louise's day-trip to Montrose turned into a two-week summer holiday and the adventure of her lifetime. On their parents' insistence that Rena stayed with her sister overnight, lodgings were found near the harbour. Much of the ensuing two weeks was spent on or around *Thorodd*. The girls joined the crew for their meals in the saloon, and the food was excellent by wartime standards. They passed the time doing minor chores, playing chess and other board games and going for walks, and they had several outings to the cinema. Einar escorted the sisters back to the lodgings every night, as often as not accompanied by Bamse. Although Louise felt awkward about intruding on their second honeymoon, Rena and Einar accepted the arrangement with good grace.

Everywhere she went on the ship, Louise was aware of the presence of Bamse, adored by all the crew and central to the life and morale of the ship. He was very evident at mealtimes, of course, hoping for scraps from the indulgent sailors. He patrolled the ship and guarded the gangway and, recognising her as an approved visitor, welcomed Louise whenever she wished to go on board.

Louise can confirm much of what has been said and written about Bamse. In the course of her holiday in Montrose she heard the accounts of the lifesaving episodes in Dundee and laughed at the stories about the stolen string of sausages and the difficulties the crew had to get him to submit to a bath! She saw his steel helmet, and from conversations with her brother-in-law she can corroborate accounts of Bamse remaining on deck during action, and that he never deserted his post despite the sound of gunfire. She saw Bamse setting off on his evening patrol of the harbour pubs to round up the crew and get them back on board before curfew. Louise remembers how well, and with what respect, she was treated by the Norwegian sailors; but even if they had behaved otherwise, Bamse would have always been extremely protective of her. She came to regard him as a truly remarkable dog and to love him as the crew did. When the fortnight came to an end, she was sad to leave Rena, her 'big brother' and everyone on board *Thorodd* who had looked after her so well, but she was particularly upset to be saying farewell to Bamse.

Jean Wallace (now Mrs Butler-Madden) was born in Montrose in 1934, so was eight years old when she first met Bamse in 1942.

The family lived in Ramsay Street, several blocks away from the docks and close to the Southesk Granary owned by John Milne & Sons, a grain and milling business where her father, Arnold Wallace, was manager. The business occupied a fine stone building, which survives in remarkably unaltered and unspoilt condition in Ferry Road, a side street that passes what used to be the back wharf of the Wet Dock where *Thorodd* frequently tied up when she was in Montrose.

Most afternoons, when school was over, Jean and her friend Marjorie MacDonald visited her father in his office at the mill. Their constant companion was Jean's faithful black Labrador, Sandy, who accompanied her everywhere, even being allowed to sit with her in her school classroom for two years! Sandy was obviously another singular dog. He had an uncanny ability to anticipate danger such as approaching air raids and would push and chivvy Jean back home when only he could sense the imminent threat. In October 1940, during the evening of the air raid when Chivers' factory was bombed, Sandy pulled Jean under the kitchen table and refused to let her move from what he perceived as a place of safety until the bombing had stopped.

As security at Montrose docks during wartime was elementary, with merely a rope looped round posts marking the barrier between the townsfolk and the military activities in the restricted port area, the two little girls and the black dog were not deterred from playing there.

Arbuthnott's boatyard had made its reputation as a builder of lifeboats, which in the context of the times were a vital requirement for the war effort. Owing to its close contacts with the Royal Navy, the boatyard also had a contract to build floating targets that were towed out to sea for RAF bombing and fighter practice. The yard lay at the seaward, or east end, of the harbour, just past the Southesk Granary, and was an adventure playground for imaginative young minds. There was a slipway where the targets were moored until called up by the Royal Navy. Jean recalls that the targets were heavily coated in tar and she regularly went home from the boatyard with hands and clothes liberally bedaubed with the sticky black substance which was almost impossible to remove completely – this at a time when rationing and clothing coupons made it difficult to buy new clothes. She still remembers the scoldings she received from her exasperated mother! When *Thorodd* was in port they often saw the familiar shape of Bamse patrolling alongside the ship. Jean kept Sandy well away, scared that the four-legged guard would decide the Labrador posed a danger and attack him. However, music unexpectedly brought the two dogs together.

During 1942 and 1943 the prisoner-of-war camp at Laurencekirk, on the inland road (A90) north from Dundee to Aberdeen, held Italian prisoners who were conscripted to work for local farms and businesses. A number of them came by lorry each morning to work at the Southesk Granary and help with the heavy labour. They were a cheerful lot who sang as they worked, and the girls and Sandy were allowed to join them during their break times. However, the choir lacked an essential member, and they appointed Jean their honorary conductor, finding her a thin cane for a conductor's baton. She was lifted onto a large sack which served as a rostrum so that the singers could follow her directions, and her indulgent father often allowed the men extra time for choir practice before returning to work. They sang mostly Italian songs, but Jean also remembers 'South of the Border (Down Mexico Way)', 'We'll Meet Again', 'The White Cliffs of Dover' and other Allied Forces' favourites rendered with a distinctive Italian lilt and passion.

The Southesk Granary was scarcely a stone's throw from the corner of the Wet Dock and within easy earshot of *Thorodd* if she was in port. More often than not, as soon as the choir tuned up for an impromptu concert, the tawny figure of Bamse appeared at the granary door, where he sat with his head cocked to one side, quietly enjoying the rich harmony. Perhaps this music was more to his taste, as Jean does not remember him ever interrupting the singers as he had done with Gerd Grieg. As Bamse was off duty as ship's sentry, Jean always felt it was safe to let Sandy out of her father's office and allow the two dogs to enjoy the music together.

The little girls would have reminded the men of their families back home in Italy, for they were very kind to them and spent their evenings in camp making them little wooden toys, rings and other novelties which they fashioned out of whatever scraps of material they could lay their hands on. Despite being prisoners, they had remarkable freedom and, when off duty in Montrose, were able to earn a few coppers selling these small items round the nearby houses. The prisoners' greatest thrill was receiving the rare delivery of a Red Cross parcel from Italy. They sat outside the granary with the girls and Sandy, sharing out the contents amongst everybody. Some of it, such as the rich cakes, seemed very exotic to the two Scottish children used to wartime restrictions. Although this abundant supply of good things was just round the corner from his ship, Bamse's remarkable nose for sniffing out free rations seems to have let him down on these occasions – perhaps he was away at sea at the time.

After the surrender of Italy in September 1943, the Italian prisoners were moved to other camps and replaced by German POWs. They were not nearly so friendly, and Arnold Wallace decided it was wise to stop the children from mixing with them.

Jean believes that her love of music dates back to those wartime experiences. She still sings, but nowadays it is with the renowned mixed-voice Kevock Choir in Edinburgh, which has performed at the Edinburgh Tattoo – so Jean has kept her musical links with the military, albeit in a peacetime setting, and without Sandy and Bamse.

The River South Esk is one of Scotland's premier salmon-fishing rivers and flows through the ancient cathedral city of Brechin on its last passage through rich farmland to Montrose and the North Sea. The inland tidal estuary of Montrose Basin moderates its flow, but it speeds up as it funnels through what used to be the north channel between the town and Rossie Island. In the 1940s this was truly an island and was linked by two bridges to the mainland. Prior to the 1970s, when the south channel was reclaimed by the port authority to create a south quay and oil support base, the outflow from Montrose Basin swept round both sides of the island.

The village of Ferryden faces north across the water to Montrose harbour. Until the mid 1960s, and certainly during the war years, the only licensed premises in the village was the Esk Hotel owned by Mrs Lily Winchester, a local personality to whom the epithets 'colourful', 'formidable', 'eccentric', and many others, could readily be attributed. When decimalisation of the UK currency was introduced in 1971, Diamond Lil, as she was universally known, refused to recognise the new decimal denominations. She continued to charge for drinks in the old currency, applying the old sterling equivalent to the new decimal coins. It seemed to work very successfully, although there was sometimes the thought that the system favoured the licensee!

In the 1940s the facilities offered by the hotel were old-fashioned, even by standards then. The men's toilet was simply the close, or alleyway, outside. Ladies brave enough to be seen in a pub in those days were directed to a 'convenience' upstairs where there was no lighting. The call for 'last orders' at night, when the bar was required by law to close, was at nine thirty, but Lil applied her own liberal interpretation of the licensing hours; a drink out of hours was rarely refused, and was often drunk in the company of the local bobby.

Knut Nicolaysen is a Norwegian merchant seaman who came to Montrose early in the North Sea oil boom of the 1970s to work at the oil support base on the former Rossie Island. He met and married Maureen and settled in Ferryden, although he has kept strong links with home through contacts in Norwegian oil-related companies and the Norwegian Seamen's Union. He first heard about Bamse, the famous dog from his homeland, from the celebrated Diamond Lil.

The story Lil told him is that during the war Montrose and Ferryden were full of servicemen and many other incomers involved with the war effort. Lil kept an accordion and a guitar behind the bar for musical customers who were brave enough to provide a bit of entertainment. To attract customers to her establishment from across the water, Lil laid on popular musical evenings featuring a guitarist who played and sang and was sometimes accompanied by an accordionist. *Thorodd*'s crew often frequented the bar, almost always in the company of their large mascot. They had a choice of waiting for the infrequent bus service which took the long way to Ferryden across Rossie Island, for a fare of tuppence, or taking the ferryboat, operated by Andrew Coull and Dan Pert, from steps beside the Wet Dock gates to the Ferryden pier just below the Esk Hotel, which cost a penny. It is a fair assumption that the thirsty sailors bundled Bamse onto the ferry for the cheaper short crossing and the earlier pint. In the bar, Bamse stretched himself out at the feet of the musicians and settled down to enjoy the singalong, and throughout the evening occasional pints of beer were poured into a bowl and laid on the floor beside him.

When it was time to return to the ship, Lil remembered the dog rounding up the crew and shepherding them out of the door. It is interesting to speculate whether they were ever in time to catch the last ferry back to the north shore or whether they always took such advantage of Lil's elastic hospitality that they had to take the long walk back. Whichever way the crew got back, it was not uncommon for Bamse to reappear at the bar on his own. Once he had relieved himself of his responsibility to his 'puppies' by returning them to the ship, he would often return for more music. He would settle once more into his favoured spot, close his eyes and let the magic of the melodies soothe his savage breast until Diamond Lil brought the evening to a close. Again, poor Gerd Grieg seems to have been the only victim of his musical annihilation for there are no stories of Bamse howling his accompaniment to the Ferryden entertainer. Diamond Lil often told Knut that Bamse was the kindest and most intelligent dog she had ever known because of the way he looked after the sailors and found his way back to the Esk Hotel.

How long it took Bamse to escort an unruly crew back to *Thorodd* and walk back again to Ferryden, a total journey of about five kilometres, can only be guessed. It must sometimes have been well after official closing time before he got back to the music, and if the bar was still open it indeed shows what a spirited disregard for the law Mrs Winchester had; but perhaps she was encouraged in this by the blind eye the law turned. Lil would eventually throw him and the rest of the diehard drinkers out into the street, and who knows at what unearthly hour he crawled into his bed in the broom cupboard, with the prospect of another day of guard duty, social calls and crew escort work ahead of him.

Bamse was welcomed wherever he went and never lacked human company, so it cannot have been loneliness that took him back to the Esk Hotel on his own. It is well documented that music has a palliative effect on animals – it has been used to relax cows in their milking parlours and induce hens in battery cages to lay more eggs. There are numerous examples of dogs responding to music, too, so the guitarist and his songs must have been the inducement for Bamse to return to the Esk Hotel in the middle of the night. His clear enjoyment of the Italian prisoners' choir – and even his participation in the Gerd Grieg concert – show that music was truly a natural stimulus, reaching deep within him and releasing a sense of wellbeing.

Reflecting on the pattern of Bamse's thought processes, it is interesting to note that, on the one hand, Bamse was able to appreciate the pleasure the music gave him, and that, on the other, when his internal clock told him it was time to engage his responsibility to return the crew to their ship, he did so, before ultimately deciding to return to the Esk Hotel for more music – a surprisingly human pattern of thought processes.

If many of the stories about Bamse seem to centre on pubs and drinking, this is because these are the memories of people still alive in Montrose and Dundee who have clear recollections of his time on shore. Bjørn Hagen's interview recorded by the

Norwegian Naval Museum in 2003 is the last known contact
with any of *Thorodd*'s crew, so it is no longer possible to find
contemporary stories, first hand, relating to his times at sea.
Taking account of the hazards of minesweeping, and the fact
that the young sailors were far from home and forbidden to
make any contact with their families, it is not surprising that
when they came on shore they often sought the familiarity and
fellowship that a bar could offer.

The Bodega Bar while he was in Dundee, the Anchor Bar
and Catzers in Ferry Street in Montrose and Diamond Lil's in
Ferryden were only some of Bamse's and his shipmates' regular
haunts. The Southesk Bar in Wharf Street in Montrose overlooks
the old, original pier, which is within the immediate harbour
area and was no further for Bamse to walk to than Catzers.
John McPherson, three years old when he came to Montrose
during the war, remembers his grandfather, who had come out
of retirement to go back to work as the maintenance engineer
at Chivers' factory, telling him that Bamse was a regular at
Harry Black's, as everyone called the Southesk Bar then, after
the publican. The Railway Bar was another 'local', and only the
Salutation Inn in Bridge Street, which was certainly well within
his sphere of operations, has no witnessed account of having
been patronised by Bamse and his drinking mates.

Anne Urquhart's family has lived in Erskine Street since the
beginning of the twentieth century. It is another street close to
the harbour and its focal point was the Railway Bar. Anne still
lives at number three, but during the war years the family lived
at number seven, next door to the Railway Bar and opposite the
Caledonian Railway Station and marshalling yard and goods
depot that serviced the dock area. For Anne, her elder sister
Agnes and her younger brother David, the railway and the

docks were their personal playground, full of excitement and interest. Arbuthnott's boatyard was only two streets away and, like Jean Wallace and Marjorie MacDonald, there was always new mischief to get up to there. Another favourite haunt was Worthies' carting stables in Meridian Street next to the docks, where they were allowed in to pet the horses.

Anne first bumped into Bamse (almost quite literally) outside the Anchor Bar in 1942 when she was six. He was the largest dog she had ever seen and shortly afterwards she was excited to see him again lying on the pavement outside the Railway Bar. He was a regular visitor to Erskine Street and whenever she met him, Bamse sat down and waited to be petted. After a while, the purpose of his appearances became evident. He was on duty, looking out for his crewmates as they left the bar, and she remembers watching him pushing and pulling the men, herding them in the general direction of the docks. He reminded Anne of one of the goods engines shunting trucks in the railway yard across the road. Surprisingly, she is the only person to have referred to Bamse's tendency to drool, or dribble, from his jowls, which is common in the St Bernard breed, and which Anne describes with a fine old-fashioned Scottish saying, 'He was aye slaverin'.' ['He was always slobbering.']

Helen Dempster was 15 when war broke out, and, as she was old enough to do so, she decided to leave school and got a job with the Montrose Co-operative Society. The family lived in River Street in Ferryden and she had to travel to the other side of the river to get to work. To save money, Helen and her two friends, Ina Dorward and Cathy Cameron, usually took the ferry. As it was a small open motorboat with no protection from the weather, the short crossing could sometimes be unpleasant. Like Alex Henderson, she was used to seeing *Thorodd* entering and leaving the port and also has vivid memories of Bamse standing at the bow beside the gun and sometimes strolling up and down the length of the ship as though he owned it.

Although *Thorodd*'s usual berth was in the Wet Dock, latterly she moored alongside the new fish quay which faced directly onto the river, and a wooden hut was placed as a shore base for the crew, with tables and chairs and a cast-iron stove for heating and cooking. The hut was not far from the old dock house and alongside steps down to the ferryboat. On a cold evening of drenching rain the three girls were huddled together against a wall, sheltering as best they could from the weather, when they heard persistent knocking from the window of the Norwegian's hut and saw a sailor gesturing to them to come inside. The sailors were cheerful and polite, delighted to have the girls' company, and offered them a very welcome cup of tea – this was the start of a routine each evening on their way home. The girls were always made most welcome by the steward in charge of the hut, but they disapproved of the condition and cleanliness of the stove. Cathy Cameron bought the steward a tin of stove black cleaner from the Co-op and showed him how to use it, and from then on the stove shone. If Bamse was on shore, the girls always had time to give him a pat and a cuddle, and they got to know him well. Surprisingly, Bamse made sure their visits were no longer than decency permitted, for he kept a lookout for the ferry and walked with them down to the steps 'like a perfect gentleman'.

Margaret McDermid has lived all her life on Wharf Street, which overlooks the original harbour frontage dating back to the 15th century. During the war she worked for Chivers, at an outstation of the factory close to the Wet Dock where *Thorodd* usually moored. She regularly saw Bamse on her way to and from work, on duty at the ship's gangway. He often crossed over to greet her and her fellow workers and was sometimes rewarded with titbits from a lunch box. She remembers his distinctive black, tan and white colouring and is now delighted that the statue erected to his memory is sited just opposite her house, so she can see him every day, looking just as she remembers him.

One of the few unsupported stories about Bamse confirms the resourceful side of his nature. A young female clerk was working diligently in an office in Meridian Street, which connects the foot of Ferry Street with the fish quay. The quiet of the room was broken by her gasps of surprise when she looked up to find an immense dog at the other side of her desk, looking at her enquiringly. Bamse had discovered that by pressing his paw on the lever handle he could open the office door. The normally strict office manager was amused by the incident and let him stay for a while, which was enough of an invitation for Bamse to become a regular caller. The young lady thought initially that he had come into the office for warmth and to escape the cold weather, but if other stories of his constant hunger are any indicator he soon made the real reason for his visits quite clear!

By 1943 Bamse's war was successfully being fought in the North Sea. On the wider front, the war was turning slowly, but inexorably, in the Allies' favour. On 2 February, after five failed months of the most desperate fighting to capture Stalingrad, the Germans surrendered to the Soviet forces with the most appalling losses on both sides. The winter weather (temperatures were as low as −30°C), starvation, frostbite and sickness, as well

Sea Dog Bamse

as the fighting, all contributed to German losses of 250,000 men, with a further 90,000 taken prisoner. The opening of a second front in North Africa put immense additional pressures on Hitler's resources. In May 1943 the complete defeat of the Italian and German forces in the North Africa Campaign brought about Allied success, with the Axis surrender and the capture of 275,000 men. The Allied invasion of Sicily, codenamed Operation Husky, was launched on 9 July. It was the largest amphibious and airborne invasion of the war to date and led to the Allied invasion of Italy and overthrow of Mussolini. On 8 September, Italy formally surrendered and Hitler lost a valuable ally.

These events brought hope and encouragement to Bamse and his crewmates on the 'little ships' as they ploughed their dangerous furrow in the sea lanes. Although they were now much more confident about the future, they were still vulnerable, for the Germans were determined to carry the war to its bitter end despite their losses on the wider stage and Britain's successes on the home front.

9

Failing Health

By 1944 Bamse was about seven years old. (There is no record of his exact date of birth.) He had amassed a range of experiences and mastered life skills far beyond those of comparable dogs. Even in his puppy months, growing up with the Hafto children, there was early evidence of his caring nature and inclination to guard and shepherd his human companions. After the dramatic flight from Norway with Erling Hafto he became the spoilt member of *Thorodd*'s crew, which he remained to his death, although it never affected his sense of responsibility or the authority he exercised over his shipmates.

He had acquitted himself with great bravery and composure in the face of hostile and clamorous enemy fire, confronting it head on alongside *Thorodd*'s bow gunner. Two men owed their lives to him; many others owed their resilience to deal with the exigencies of wartime conditions to his comforting presence when they needed it. He had a strong sense of fair play, fearing no one and never hesitating to intervene in drunken brawls. Music, football and travel had broadened his outlook, and he had become the most sociable and companionable of dogs, showing unconditional affection and consideration for almost everyone, young and old, with whom he came into contact.

However, little if any mention is made of Bamse's faults, and it would be unrealistic to think he had none. Greed was perhaps one of his weaknesses. He seems to have been constantly hungry, and it is evident that a lot of his off-duty time was spent calling at regular sources of extra food, where he was rarely disappointed. While a dog can be trained to feed only at specific times and from a particular bowl, as often as not Bamse's daily timetable must have been irregular, and there may well have been occasions when, if he did not look after himself, he might not have been fed at all. In any event, with so many benevolent friends ready to spoil him with scraps and other treats, it would be surprising if he had had the discipline to self-regulate his feeding.

For all his goodwill towards his human companions, Bamse seems to have been ambivalent about other animals that invaded his territory, although this might be considered more a natural response than a fault. There are stories that he did not like canine competition. Fritz Egge recounted an anecdote about a bulldog that was ship's mascot of a British minesweeper which tied up alongside *Thorodd* in Dundee. Whenever the two dogs met on the quayside they growled and showed their teeth to each other and had to be restrained. Eventually Bamse managed to corner the bulldog in a coal bunker and brought their private war to a fitting conclusion. He emerged victorious from the encounter, black with coal dust, upholding the pride of the Norwegian Navy against the British bulldog, and the defeated combatant slunk back to its own ship. 'In triumph he returned to *Thorodd* looking more like a chimney sweep's brush than a pedigree hound,' remembers Fritz. The horrified crew tried to stop him coming up the gangway, determined not to let him bring the filth aboard. Bamse, however, was not to be stopped, and on reaching the deck he went to find a bucket of water. He sat down beside it and simply waited to be given a bath. Of course there were no volunteers for the job, and from the bridge a directive had to be issued for an 'Order of the Bath!'

Unwittingly, another dog called Nikken came on board *Thorodd* when Bamse's attention was distracted. The unsuspecting visitor got short shrift when a jealous Bamse chased him ashore again. The crew were embarrassed by this stain on their hospitality, and Bamse was hauled up on a charge before the captain, Lieutenant Oscar Jensen, who confined him to the ship. There are two versions of what happened when he was released from confinement. The first is that incarceration gave him time to kindle his revenge, and as soon as he was released he sought out Nikken and squared his account with him comprehensively. The other is that he went ashore and, in a show of canine camaraderie, allowed Nikken back on board where he became a member of the crew for a short period. This latter story is supported by another recounting that when *Thorodd* sailed into port, probably at Montrose, Bamse and Nikken became increasingly excited as she approached her berth and both stood in the bows barking so uncontrollably that the captain's orders could not be heard. Oscar Jensen had to shout at Bamse in Norwegian – 'Hold kejft!' – and 'Shut up!' at Nikken in order to make himself understood and get them both to keep quiet.

Cats were not greatly favoured by Bamse either. A photograph shows the dog in the company of four sailors, one of them with his girlfriend on his arm, and another holding the ship's cat. It seems that Katt was tolerated for a time but its luck ran out when it irritated Bamse after a particularly gruelling minesweeping operation when he was suffering the after-effects of seasickness. Bamse lost patience with Katt and lunged at the animal, barking loudly. Fortunately *Thorodd* was in port, and Katt jumped ship and was not seen again. On the photograph, another dog's head and shoulders peep out from between the knees of two of the sailors, and it is tempting to think that this was Nikken, with whom Bamse had made his peace. If so, it is difficult to identify Nikken's breed; there is a suggestion of whippet, but perhaps he – or she – was just a harbour stray of indeterminate parentage.

It is good to know, however, that for a dog who spent so much of his adult life in a male-dominated environment, Bamse found time for love on at least one occasion, for he left his genealogical pawprint on Dundee. Sailors being sailors, it should be expected that Bamse played the field with the lady dogs from time to time. Fritz Egge's is the only known account of his paternity, and he gave only the briefest details, but Bamse definitely sired a litter of puppies in circumstances which suggest it was not a planned union. History does not say what breed the bitch was, but as no mention is ever made of another St Bernard in Bamse's life (they were not a common breed in Scotland in the war years), she may have been a mongrel living half-wild round the harbour area. Not all the puppies survived, but running around the streets of Dundee today there must still be dogs carrying the noble DNA of 'the largest dog of the Allied Forces'.

Meanwhile the war in Europe raged on unabated, with Allied Forces continuing to make significant inroads into the Axis defence. The amphibious landings on the Anzio beaches, south of Rome on Italy's western coast, in January 1944 were costly in terms of Allied losses. However, they were immensely successful in tying down significant numbers of German frontline troops, which created a huge drain on German troop reserves, equipment and materials. Planning and training continued throughout 1944 in the build-up to Operation Overlord, which culminated in the largest seaborne invasion in history. On 6 June 1944, D-Day, up to 7,000 ships of every description crossed the English

Channel to land 156,000 American and other Allied troops on the Normandy beaches, codenamed Sword, Juno, Gold, Omaha and Utah, between Le Havre and Cherbourg, to open up the second front. The Norwegian Merchant Navy which, at the outbreak of war, was the fourth largest and one of the most efficient merchant shipping fleets in the world, made a major contribution to the Normandy landings. While *Thorodd* was not part of these operations, minesweepers were a vital component in the vanguard fleet, providing a safe sea corridor, 32 kilometres wide, for the main attacking fleet.

By this time, Bamse's life was entering its final stage. *Thorodd's* main operational berth was now at Montrose, and Bamse had become as firmly embedded in the life of the port and people of the town as he had been in Dundee. His reputation had spread throughout Europe, and he had been adopted as mascot, first by all the Free Norwegian Forces, and subsequently by other Allied troops. There are apparently reliable stories of postcards with an image of his head, wearing his Norwegian Navy cap, being exchanged between troops all over Europe at Christmas and Easter. Frustratingly, no surviving examples of the cards can be traced, although extensive enquiries have been made to various sources such as the Norwegian royal family's archives and even the Norwegian Postcard Club. Whatever the truth is about these cards, it is clear from the research undertaken in writing this book that by 1944 Bamse had become the iconic figure that he is known to be today.

Nothing further has been said about Halldis Hafto and the four children since their introduction at the beginning of the book. They remained in the family home in Honningsvåg when Erling sailed to Lerwick, and, in common with the families of the rest of *Thorodd's* crew, a curtain of silence descended between them and Erling. As is known now, the embargo on communication meant that some mothers died without knowing whether their sons survived the war, while fathers and husbands like Erling lived through the war not knowing what the fate of their families was.

The Norwegians suffered enormous privations under the German occupation of their country. Norway remained legally at war with Germany, with resistance directed by the *de jure* government, in exile in London, and most Norwegians took the view that hopeless resistance was better than craven appeasement of the hated occupier. Vidkun Quisling's attempts immediately after the German occupation to declare himself prime minister on behalf of the Nazis were immediately quashed by King Haakon from London, and he was promptly sacked by Hitler as no longer being of any political use to him. Although reinstated in 1942 as Minister President to lead a puppet government, his efforts to persuade the professional classes and the trade unions, in particular, to take a lead in supporting the phoney regime failed completely. The Norwegians turned their backs on Quisling's attempts to impose Nazification on their country and refused to reach any sort of compromise over their national independence.

For five years Norway effectively lost contact with the outside world. The Nazis imposed a brutal martial law, relying on fear and terror to implement it. A strong Norwegian underground movement responded with armed resistance, industrial sabotage and civil disobedience. Summary executions, internment in concentration camps, labour conscription and police purges merely stiffened Norwegian defiance. However much Erling Hafto may have known of all of this through his contacts within the Norwegian naval command, there was little that he could realistically do to help his family, other than to fight the war to the best of his endeavours.

In 1943 Erling Hafto was taken off his seagoing duties as captain of *Nordkapp*, which had been operating in the seas round Iceland, promoted to *orlogskaptein*, or commander, and transferred to the Norwegian naval staff in London. His previous naval experience and extensive knowledge of the northern polar waters were invaluable to the war effort. His daughter Vigdis believes that he attended the minesweeping school at Port Edgar for orientation or other instruction before he took up his post in London. There is every reason to believe that while he was at Port Edgar he had contact with his former crew members on *Thorodd*. Vigdis has confirmed that her father took every opportunity to keep up to date with Bamse's welfare (and that of his former command and her crew, too) and knew much about Bamse's exploits throughout the course of the war. Bearing in mind his emotional parting from Bamse when he left Port Edgar to take command of *Nordkapp*, and his insistence that he would return for his family's pet, it would have been surprising if it had been otherwise. This continuing contact has a sequential relevance to Bamse's story and the perpetuation of his memory in the posthumous award in 2006 of the PDSA Gold Medal.

PDSA is the United Kingdom's leading veterinary charity providing free veterinary treatment to sick and injured animals belonging to owners who are unable to pay for treatment. The People's Dispensary for Sick Animals was founded by Mrs Maria Dickin. She was a remarkable Edwardian lady who was too intelligent and energetic to be satisfied with the narcissistic life of a society hostess and so filled the gap with social work in London's East End. She was horrified by the human poverty she encountered, as well as being haunted by the silent suffering of the injured and sick animals she saw scavenging in the streets or chained up in backyards, and the working animals crippled and lamed by ill-treatment and overwork.

Maria opened her first People's Dispensary for Sick Animals of the Poor in a Whitechapel basement on 17 November 1917. Above the door was a notice:

BRING YOUR SICK ANIMALS.
DO NOT LET THEM SUFFER.
ALL ANIMALS TREATED.
ALL TREATMENT FREE.

The free service was such an instant success that Maria was encouraged in her vision to improve the dreadful state of animal health and set up veterinary dispensaries throughout the country. In due course, she extended her work abroad.

In January 1943 PDSA instituted the Allied Forces Mascot Club to acknowledge the important contribution of service animals and 'famous mascots on all the battlefronts whose presence played an important part in maintaining morale'. Membership was open to animals serving with the Allied Forces, and the aims of the club met with widespread approval. A heterogeneous assortment of animals and birds including dogs, cats, monkeys, a rat and a mongoose, chickens and canaries, were proposed for membership. Erling Hafto was posted to London around this time and found that his office was close to PDSA Head Office at 14 Clifford Street in the city's West End. He got to know Dorothea St Hill Bourne (another remarkable woman), who was secretary of the Mascot

Club, and he proposed Bamse for membership in May 1944. Not surprisingly, his application was successful, and Bamse was enrolled on 1 June 1944. As a result, he appears in several books written after the war in tribute to the role of animals in wartime.

The formation of the Allied Forces Mascot Club highlighted the large number of examples of conspicuous acts of gallantry displayed in action by animals serving with the armed forces, not only in past conflicts, but particularly in the course of World War II. Later in 1943, in order to honour these animals further, Maria Dickin instituted the PDSA Dickin Medal, PDSA's oldest and most famous award, which is recognised internationally as the animals' Victoria Cross. The world is still troubled by wars which British troops and animals play their part in, and the PDSA Dickin Medal continues to be awarded for acts of lifesaving gallantry.

Although Bamse has sometimes been credited with the award of the PDSA Dickin Medal, this has, in fact, been an erroneous assumption. The Mascot Club was wound up at the end of the war and its records transferred to the Imperial War Museum, and PDSA lost sight of Bamse. He had not been nominated for, or awarded, a PDSA Dickin Medal, and PDSA had no reason to keep any further record of him. Had it not been for Erling Hafto's posting to London it is unlikely that Bamse would have even been nominated for the Allied Forces Mascot Club. The club was set up in London some 18 months before Bamse's death, and no accounts have been found in the regional Scottish newspapers about mascots of Scottish units being accepted for membership. Norwegian sailors on a small ship in a small port on the east coast of Scotland would have had little opportunity to learn about the club, let alone know how to make application for Bamse's membership, and it was only Hafto's timely posting to London that provided the opportunity to recognise the dog's contribution to the war effort. It was brief recognition at the time, but it did reinforce the importance of acknowledging the contribution animals made to morale when men's spirits were low.

Awards continue to be approved by PDSA Council and the charity carries on its essential core work of free treatment for eligible pet owners. It looks forward to its centenary as it expands its support services of PDSA PetAid hospitals, promotes responsible pet care and fitness, runs a children's club called PDSA Pet Protectors and provides speakers for community talks. It took more than 60 years for Bamse's story to resurface, and PDSA's public recognition, with the award of the PDSA Gold Medal, of his place amongst inspirational wartime animals is a fitting tribute to the dog, adding legitimacy to his incredible story.

Ronald Webster, who was part of a large family of 13 living in Montrose at 63 Garrison Road (another street close to the harbour), knew Bamse only as the friendly dog he met on *Thorodd*. He was eight years old when war broke out, and even at that young age he was a busy lad with a daily newspaper delivery round. With so many at home, he and his sister Irene, just one year younger than him, played outside as much as possible. Like other children living nearby, they treated the harbour area as their personal recreational area, ducking under the symbolic rope barrier to cut through the docks on their way to and from Southesk School.

Ronald and Irene first met Bamse on a morning in the autumn of 1943 when the two youngsters saw him on his daily patrol up and down the deck of *Thorodd*. Several friendly sailors were on deck too and they waved across to the two youngsters. Ever keen to earn an extra penny or two of pocket money, Ronald shouted, 'Hey mister, do you need any messages [shopping] today?'

'You wait,' came the reply in a strong, foreign accent. After a few minutes the sailor reappeared with a list to be taken to MacFarlane's grocery, quite a large establishment at the top of Castle Street, which even in wartime was able to keep a delivery van on the road. After this first errand, Ronald got into the habit of calling at the ship on his way to or from school and became the ship's regular message boy.

The sailors were appreciative of his help and rewarded him with small tips of money or gifts of chocolate and sweets. When he and Irene were invited to go on board they were entertained in the wardroom with cups of tea along with biscuits and cake, which were real treats in the wartime years. If *Thorodd* was in port at weekends an even greater treat for them was to be invited to join the sailors for a Saturday lunch of mince, potatoes and vegetables – sometimes a bigger meal than they got at home. The Norwegians were all very kind to them, and several of them spoke very good English. There were no objections from the officers to the children being on the ship; as in the case of Rena Andersen's second honeymoon, the presence of civilians and children on board when *Thorodd* was tied up in port was perfectly acceptable.

Ronald and Irene got to know Bamse well; he was always on, or rarely far from, the ship and spent a lot of time in his wicker basket out on deck. Occasionally he accompanied Ronald on the half-mile journey to the grocer's shop, but by the spring of

1944 the big dog's health was beginning to fail. He was losing weight and becoming increasingly breathless, and as time passed he became clearly unwell, scarcely leaving the ship.

St Bernard dogs, in common with most large breeds, are not long-lived animals and their average life expectancy is about eight years. Their hearts frequently cannot cope with the demands of their heavily built frames, and from the descriptions of his health towards the end of his life, it seems he exhibited the classic symptoms of heart failure. His condition would have deteriorated and there would have been a change in his personality as the strain on his heart made day-to-day living more and more difficult and uncomfortable. The crew were very concerned and attentive, and Ronald remembers being on board several times when the local vet, Mr Willie Rice, was called to the ship to attend to Bamse, on one occasion giving him an injection.

Unaware of his failing heart, some people thought that Bamse had not been treated as well as he might have been. Some even went so far as to accuse *Thorodd*'s crew of being neglectful of the dog. Robert Whyte was aged 14 at the time of Bamse's death and only became aware of the dog in the last few months of his life. His mother Hilda ran a small grocer's shop in Commerce Street, near the docks, and Robert helped out in the shop during his free time. He describes a very different Bamse from the one most other people remember. His only clear memory was of a thin, unkempt dog calling at the shop looking for a hand-out. He was obviously hungry, for when Robert held out a broken bridie (a traditional Scottish mutton pasty) Bamse, he recalls, 'Nearly took my hand with it!' This is at odds with previous anecdotes about Bamse being a rather fastidious eater. The dog by this stage was clearly unwell; he had lost a lot of weight – 'thin as a greyhound' was Robert's comment – and his coat was in poor condition.

Several others have confirmed Bamse's deteriorating appearance in the latter months of his life, maintaining that his suffering had been prolonged unnecessarily and that, in unsentimental terms, he should have been put down at an earlier stage than he actually was. James MacDonald worked at Arbuthnott's boatyard during 1944 and remembers seeing Bamse wandering rather aimlessly around the docks, or on *Thorodd*, gulping down any raw fish passing fishermen threw him. Bamse was in a feeble state by then – 'The dog was just done,' he recalls.

These narrators were not aware of Bamse's failing heart, the cause of his weight loss, the breathlessness and his change of character. Nor were they aware of his previous exploits and heroism. To them he was simply a sick and neglected animal at the end of his years, and for many years they remained sceptical about the stories of his life that emerged. They are no longer here to defend themselves against such criticism, but it is inconceivable that the Norwegians ceased caring about Bamse as his health worsened, and this is borne out by Ronald Webster's eyewitness account. Bamse was the embodiment of everything the sailors held dear. He was their mascot, their uncompromising source of strength in the dark days, and their friend and shipmate in the good days. They had even been prepared to confront Erling Hafto, and defy higher authority if need be, to ensure their hero stayed with them.

However, as his heart gradually gave up, Bamse's end drew near. There are no veterinary notes to refer to, and based on what little information is available, only an educated guess can be made as to exactly what brought about Bamse's demise. St Bernards, as a breed, have a tendency to suffer from a congenital or inherent disorder called dilated cardiomyopathy, the cause of congestive heart failure. The underlying disorder is a thinned and poor heart muscle, which means that the heart is big and flabby and does not work efficiently. His lungs would have been so awash with fluid that his breathing would have been severely impaired. As he weakened he would have curtailed his activities and become increasingly confined to the ship. The final stage would have been the onset of 'friendly pneumonia', so called because it hastens the inevitable end, and for which, in the wartime 1940s, there was no available treatment.

Duncan Strang gave a graphic account of Bamse's final moments. Duncan had been discharged from active service as the result of a war wound received in 1943 and had returned to his hometown of Montrose early in 1944. He got a job working at the docks and, living close by, got in the habit of taking a shortcut from home to work past the inner Wet Dock where *Thorodd* was a regular sight. As ever, Bamse patrolled up and down the ship, guarding the gangway very effectively against all comers except the ship's company. 'No one would argue with him!' was Duncan's wry comment. He also clearly remembered the sight of Bamse pulling drunk crew members out of the Anchor Bar at the foot of Ferry Street and shepherding them back to the ship.

On 1 July 1944 *Thorodd* had tied up at Montrose for what turned out to be the last time. Like Bamse, the ship was 'just done', and she was to undergo repairs at Arbuthnott's yard in an effort to extend her working life. On the afternoon of Saturday 22 July, Duncan was walking from the Customs House direction, eastwards along the dockside past a wooden coal shed (now long-demolished but known then, prosaically, as 'the sheddie'!) between Arbuthnott's boatyard and the Wet

Dock. A small crowd had gathered by the side of the shed about twenty paces from *Thorodd*'s gangway, and Duncan went to investigate. At the centre of the gathering lay Bamse, collapsed, breathless and obviously near his life's end. He must have made one instinctive last effort to go ashore on his rounds, and his big heart had finally had enough. He was surrounded by distraught members of *Thorodd*'s crew and also some dockworkers. Willie Rice the vet had been called and was on his knees beside him. Willie already knew his patient and was well aware of his heart condition; and now pneumonia had set in. At best it might have been possible to prolong his life for a day or two but he would have known immediately that the kindest thing to do was to bring Bamse's suffering to a speedy end. A syringe was produced and Duncan witnessed Bamse being humanely put to sleep, finally relieved of his suffering. A stillness descended on the quayside as a sense of loss and desolation filled every one of Bamse's shipmates. Each felt the isolation and loneliness normally associated with the death of a parent or other close relative. Their lives had been enriched by the incredible 'teddy bear', and each now felt heartsore with his passing.

Ronald had enjoyed his rewarding job as *Thorodd*'s messenger boy for eight or nine months, but on 23 July 1944 it shockingly all came to an end when he made one of his regular visits to the docks to see if *Thorodd*'s crew had any errands for him to run. As he approached the ship he sensed that something was out of the ordinary. As well as some sailors, a number of civilian workers were gathered about, heads bowed and talking quietly. Ronald pressed forward. 'Whit are ye lookin' for?' asked a stranger. He explained that he was the ship's semi-official message boy. 'There'll be nae messages today,' came the reply, 'the dog's deid – died yesterday'. Overwhelmed, Ronald melted away, hurrying home to tell his family.

Learning that Bamse's funeral would be the following day, Ronald went down early to the docks to ensure he missed nothing. Others had the same idea too, as there were many Norwegian sailors standing on board *Thorodd* and on the quayside. One report of the day says that seamen from six Norwegian vessels attended the funeral, which suggests that sailors who had known him travelled up from Dundee. A growing crowd of other servicemen and civilians was also assembling and the mood was sombre. After a while, there was activity on *Thorodd*, and a party of sailors advanced to the gangplank carrying a short ladder on their shoulders, on which, very obviously, lay Bamse, for his long tail hung down beneath the navy greatcoat which covered his body. They carried him down the gangway and transferred him onto a flat hand-barrow which was lent for the occasion by Alecky Brannen, a local worthy who used the barrow in connection with his business selling fresh fish round the houses. This was no ordinary hand-cart. David Oswald, brought up on Rossie Island, remembers it as an exuberant work of art. It was painted bright green with red handles and wheel spokes, all picked out in detail with brightly coloured sea shells. Alecky kept it spotlessly clean with the fish beautifully presented. (Once again, how the intertwining strands of this story repeat themselves – Bamse's story started with a handcart and ended with another). Bamse was too long for the cart and his tail still hung out underneath the coat, on top of which his naval cap had now been placed. (There is no record of what happened to his steel helmet and his seaman's collar.)

The funeral parade assembled and came to some order. Leading off ahead of Alecky Brannen's barrow was a party of about 20 sailors carrying the ladder, some shovels, a pickaxe, sheets, blankets and a Norwegian flag. Following on was a larger party of sailors from the other Norwegian ships along with other servicemen. Finally there was a considerable crowd of civilians, both adults and children. The parade passed the familiar Southesk Granary, scene of happy musical memories for Bamse, before marching south down Ferry Road and east via Cobden Street. The procession arrived at sand dunes overlooking the mouth of the River South Esk and the entrance to Montrose harbour, sights that had been familiar to Bamse standing in *Thorodd's* bow as she steamed gently upriver to her berth.

At the chosen site, the burial party set to work to dig a grave in the soft sand. Ronald watched from a distance, standing on his own, and he recollects that it took a long time for them to complete their task, which is scarcely surprising given the size of grave needed for such a large animal. Word had quickly gone round the town in the two days since Bamse's death and more and more townsfolk arrived at the graveside until there was a crowd of several hundred spread out amongst the dunes. It was school holiday time and numbers of children, many organised in school groups, attended the service. Jessie Paton and her classmates from Southesk School were amongst the mourners closest to the graveside, and she remembers she saw and heard little of the service because, like many of the children, tears were streaming down her cheeks. It has been suggested that 800 children lined the funeral route, but local opinion does not confirm this, although a large number of schoolchildren were certainly present.

The long, deep pit was lined with sheets and Bamse's body

was transferred back onto the ladder, which was lowered on ropes into the grave. He was laid out with his head facing northeast, in the direction of Norway, and two pillows were placed under his head. Finally, a clean white naval blanket was laid over him. The Norwegian sailors lined up in two parties, one on each side of the open grave, and Captain Oscar Jensen led a short burial service, conducted in Norwegian. Prayers were said and the sailors sang a hymn. Afterwards, the burial party stepped forward and filled in the grave. The solemnities of the day completed, the sailors returned to their ships, and the other mourners dispersed.

It marked the close of the final chapter in the lives of two old warhorses which had shared a war's duration of adventures. *Thorodd* remained tied up at Montrose until 2 September 1944 when the decision was taken that she was no longer sufficiently seaworthy to merit the further repairs that had been proposed for her. *Thorodd* and Bamse had been on their last legs together, and, perhaps fittingly, they bowed out together.

Inevitably after so many years there are variations and discrepancies in people's memories of Bamse's funeral. For a long time it was generally accepted that he was buried in a full-sized coffin, but Ronald Webster is adamant that no coffin was used. Although they perhaps could have asked sympathetic joiners at Arbuthnott's boatyard to knock together a cheap box of deal planking, a professionally made coffin would probably have been too great an expense for the sailors. As it was, Bamse was buried more fittingly in the style of sailors buried at sea.

This raises the question of why he was not buried at sea. The reasons may have been practical: *Thorodd* was tied up for yet more repairs; there was no indication of when she would return to sea; and how would the big body be dealt with until she did? So why was another ship not asked to carry out the formalities? As there are no surviving members of *Thorodd*'s crew to answer the question, it would be gratifying to think that by burying him in Scotland the Norwegians hoped to preserve a little piece of Norway in a corner of Bamse's second homeland, where he had spent five mostly very happy years. Whatever their intention, they succeeded in creating a place of pilgrimage. Bamse's grave has been honoured on a number of occasions by formal visits of ships of the Royal Norwegian Navy which have sailed into Montrose and whose crews have visited his resting place to pay tribute to his memory. In so doing, they have honoured the forthright, personal relationship between dog and sailors which was summed up by Fritz Egge – 'Like a brother we loved him, and he returned the love many times over.'

The resurgence of his story now will ensure that his burial place continues to be at the heart of the special relationship between the Norwegian and Scottish people. The first of several crosses erected on the grave was fashioned by Einar Andersen who collected scrap wood from around the harbour to make it. He relates in a Norwegian book entitled (in translation) *The Ship's Dog Bamse and Other Dogs* by Otto Opstad: 'I was present at the moment of Bamse's death. Bamse looked at me with friendly eyes just before he died. The same day I went to the docks and found some wooden materials and made a cross. I carved in the name Bamse with my knife.' Einar's simple cross, hurriedly made, appears in a photograph taken after the funeral with some of *Thorodd*'s crew holding the Norwegian flag as a backdrop. 'BAMSE' is roughly carved on the cross piece, and is

flanked by two painted representations of the Norwegian flag.
The upper section of the upright piece has the date of his death,
22–7–44, carved into it and surmounted by another depiction
of the Norwegian flag.

During Bamse's illness Einar deliberately found ways to
prevent his sister-in-law Louise from visiting Montrose, because
he knew she would be upset to see the dog in his saddened
state. When he died, Einar telephoned his wife Rena (who was
back again in Dundee and helping with the family business) to
break the news to her sister. The following morning, the two
sisters caught the train to Montrose, but its arrival was delayed,
and they arrived too late for the start of the funeral service.
Louise never forgot the emotion of the occasion, and when she
subsequently read the account of Bamse's death in Evelyn le
Chêne's *Silent Heroes: The Bravery and Devotion of Animals in
War*, she felt that the author had accurately captured the spirit
of the dog in his death:

> The shock and grief were palpable and sincere. It was, as one person
> described it, as if the silence that descended upon the little vessel
> was a special silence. A great emptiness was suddenly there. No
> member of the *Thorodd*'s crew was unaffected. Grown men who
> had stoically endured a cruel war, separation from their families,
> grave losses and exile from their country, cried openly. This was
> a very personal bereavement to them. Grief was not confined to
> the *Thorodd*. It was instantly echoed far and wide, in the naval
> depots, on visiting ships, on the streets of Dundee and Montrose,
> in the taverns and on the buses, and in all the local schools. There
> could not have been a more loving bond between two peoples, the
> Norwegians and the Scots, than that which Bamse had created.

Sixty-two years after the funeral, Louise was driven to Montrose
by her daughter to visit Bamse's statue after its unveiling by

HRH Prince Andrew. As she was helped out of the car, she was struck by the statue's likeness to the original dog. She put out her hand to pat Bamse and was overcome with the vividness of her memories of the honeymoon summer, and burst into uncontrollable floods of tears.

10

The Sands of Time

The mountainous fjordlands of Norway contrast greatly with the extensive beaches and sand dunes of the central east coast of Scotland. Passing the time with a small ball and a stick in these dunes, or links, as they have been known since the Middle Ages, gave birth to the game of golf, now indelibly associated with the famous championship courses at St Andrews and Carnoustie. Amongst the oldest links courses in Scotland are those of St Andrews, Musselburgh, North Berwick, Dornoch, Crail and Montrose. There is much debate in golfing circles as to which has been there longest, and currently it is claimed that Montrose links are the fifth oldest in the world. The game has been played there since at least 1562, when James Melville, the famous cleric and reformer born in 1556, was taught as a child 'how to use the glubb for goff'.

Bamse was laid to rest just south of the historic golf links. The grave is unobtrusively situated amid the dunes on the north bank of the River South Esk, about a kilometre away from the docks, overlooking the river itself. In spite of the marram grasses and other dune vegetation which bind the sand into position, easterly storms carry clouds of stinging, shifting sand from the adjoining beach across the area, threatening to obliterate the site. Further up the east coast at Findhorn, in a river-mouth situation very similar to that of Montrose, the entire village disappeared in storms during the 17th century, never to be seen again. But Bamse's grave has never been lost to the sands, and the story of its survival is one of the remarkable aspects of his memory.

The grave was marked by the sailors with Einar Andersen's plain cross, but later the same day it took on a new appearance. Anne Urquhart, then aged 10, had watched the start of Bamse's funeral procession, but had been unable to follow it because her mother needed her to do some shopping. Upset at missing the service, Anne and a group of school friends went to the dunes and found the cross and the freshly heaped sand. As they stood round, each lost in their own memories of the dog who had been so friendly to children, they had an idea. Going down to the beach, they gathered colourful, smooth pebbles and shells with which they edged and decorated the borders of the grave. Finally they went through the dunes gathering bunches of the wild flowers found there in abundance in July. These they laid reverently on Bamse's last resting place.

Anne and her friends initiated the maintenance of Bamse's grave, which continues to this day. The other Anne, Anne Ross, whose baby had been 'menaced' by Bamse's sudden emergence from the Caledonia Bar's back alley, and who became such a friend to him afterwards, became the self-appointed custodian of his grave. Over the next 20 years, she faithfully visited it each week to keep it tidy. Her daughter, Moira, still follows in the footsteps of her mother, regularly going to the grave. It became a custom for Montrose folk, passing by while out walking, to pick up a polished stone from the beach, or a beautiful seashell, and lay it on the grave. Posies of flowers brightened the site, and sometimes a dog, whilst being walked, would leave its stick at the grave, in unknowing tribute to one of its kind. All of this, over the years, could have resulted in the area becoming untidy if left untended, but Anne ensured that it was always kept in order.

Another regular visitor who helped look after the grave was young Andrew Mearns, son of the harbour pilot, also named Andrew, who had so often guided *Thorodd* into port. Born into a seagoing life, Andrew was given his first boat when he was nine. The ancient 10-foot clinker-built rowing boat, known as *Leaky Nellie*, was his pride and joy, and he spent many happy hours sailing in her. He rigged up a mast with a broken oar and a ketch sail made out of a potato sack. Launching his magnificent vessel from the foreshore, he battled with the fast-flowing tides and currents of the River South Esk.

Andrew was 11 when Bamse was buried in the sand dunes opposite his Ferryden home. His father told him tales about the dog and about the burial, and these so inspired his curiosity that he decided to row across the river and visit the grave. He was moved by the experience and started to return on a regular basis every week or two. He tidied up the site if it was necessary and always took a few moments to think about the famous dog. It was an example of unusual devotion for a young boy to make such visits, which continued for three years until he left school aged 14 and, as his father had done before him, went to sea and to the fishing.

There were many others, friends of Bamse and of the crew of the *Thorodd*, who visited and helped to maintain the unassuming memorial. The neglected graves and memorials of humans quickly fall into disrepair, and the resting place of a mere dog might have been expected to share this fate. By 1945 the terrible war was over; hundreds of servicemen had left Montrose, and hundreds separated from their families for five long years had returned. There had been disruption, destruction and death, and it was time to put all of this behind them. However, despite the eagerness to move on with their lives, Bamse was not forgotten.

Thorodd is not remembered as well as her ship's dog; indeed she has been remembered largely only because of Bamse. At the time of his death, the ship was lying in Montrose for repairs. Already much altered during the pre-war years, her wartime role had necessitated substantial refitting, and she had needed to be re-ballasted in order to restore lost stability. Her task of minesweeping had kept her at sea for long periods in the hostile environment of the North Sea. Chief Engineer Anders Larsen, who stayed with her from the beginning of the war until she was finally laid up must have realised latterly that as Bamse's life drew to a close, *Thorodd*'s operational serviceability was coming to an end too. Even after a further two months of modification at Arbuthnott's yard she was deemed unfit for further minesweeping duties. Under the command of Lieutenant Oscar Jensen, she cast off for the last time at Montrose, heading down the river, past Scurdy Ness lighthouse and out to sea. It was a sad last voyage down the familiar route to Dundee, where she bade a farewell to sister ships KNM *Nordhav II*, KNM *Syrian*, and KNM *Bortind*, with whom she had served throughout the war. The Norwegian sailors were not only losing *Thorodd*, but they had also just lost their mascot Bamse, who they had all known and loved so much.

Thorodd headed south towards the familiar waters of the Firth of Forth, where she was laid up at the harbour at Burntisland, which lies on the north shore, opposite Edinburgh. So much had happened in the years since *Thorodd* had arrived at Port Edgar and she had undergone her transformation for her minesweeping duties. Then the war had been all but lost; now it was all but won, and *Thorodd* and her crew had played their parts in this turn of fortune. The crew were dispersed to other ships of the Norwegian Navy, and *Thorodd* languished at Burntisland for nearly a year.

Nordhav II suffered an even worse fate just two months before the end of the war. On 10 March 1945, she was on station 18 kilometres off Arbroath, close to the Bell Rock marked by the famous Bell Rock lighthouse between Dundee and Montrose. She was hit by a torpedo from the German submarine *U-714* and sank rapidly. The commander, four Norwegian crew and one British sailor were lost. Seventeen survivors, of whom five were wounded, were picked up by *Syrian* and returned to Dundee.

Though less tragic than that of *Nordhav II*, *Thorodd*'s finale was still dramatic. On 8 May 1945 the Allies celebrated Victory in Europe (VE) Day. It was time to think of home, and in August *Thorodd* sailed back to Norway with a skeleton crew of naval personnel to be returned to her previous owners. Again she languished, unsuited now for any civilian task, until 1947 when she underwent yet a further conversion back to commercial use, and was used variously as a seine-net fishing boat and as a freighter. On 6 October 1955 whilst sailing in heavy weather in Olsofjorden with a freight of pyrites, the cargo shifted, and the ship began to list heavily. She began to take on water, and the crew were rescued without loss of life before she finally sank. She now lies on her port side, in about 20 metres of water, to the south of the picturesque old harbour town of Risør and is still visible through the clear waters on a calm day.

Erling Hafto epitomised the Norwegian seafaring tradition, but above all he was a home-loving man. In 1931 he had given up a promising career at sea to settle his family at Honningsvåg. The war had returned him to seagoing duties, which totally disrupted his family life. For five anxious years he had hardly known whether the wife and children he had left behind had survived or what had become of them. He had endured a long and unkind war, but had made a valuable contribution to the war effort, from his command of *Thorodd,* and then *Nordkapp,* to his promotion to *orlogskaptein* and transfer to the Norwegian naval staff in London, where he had worked in naval intelligence, particularly with regards to mine-clearance operations.

During the build-up to the D-Day operations, he had directed the Norwegian divisions of the minesweeper forces, desperately and successfully keeping the English Channel free from mine threat, and for this task he received a special commendation from Allied High Command. A year later, in May 1945, with the Nazi hold on Norway coming to an end, he was amongst the early arrivals of liberating forces at Trømso, where he was to direct mine clearance after the war. But where was his family? What had become of them? When would they see each other again?

Already rumours were being confirmed by intelligence about what had happened in the far north. Life had been very hard for those who lived under the German occupation, particularly for those who were known to have a family member fighting in the Free Norwegian Forces, as had been the case with the

Hafto family. A steadfast, brave woman protecting her four young children, Halldis had had many confrontations and stand-offs with the oppressors. Hunger and cold had been equally unwelcome enemies. In mid 1944, news of Russian advances into Finland had been followed by the retreat in September of German forces into northern Norway. What happened in the autumn of 1944 had gone beyond the dreadful expediency of military strategy to acts of dreadful revenge and spite. On 13 October the commander of German forces in Finnmark, General Lothar Rendulic, had ordered the forced eviction of the entire population and the burning of every building in Finnmark and North Troms. When the people had been reluctant to obey, a *Führerbefehl* (a personal command from Hitler, to be obeyed on pain of death) had been issued on 28 October, ensuring that the orders were carried out with ruthless efficiency. Tens of thousands of people had been driven into small boats and ordered to make their way south, where they had been obliged to throw themselves onto the charity of their already suffering countrymen. Quite a few had decided to try to stay, thinking that the war would shortly be over. Escaping the German round-up, they had fled to remote areas, living in caves and abandoned mines. Some had resorted to the old Viking practice of turning their boats upside down and living underneath them. How they survived the winter of 1944–45 is almost beyond imagination.

If the Germans did not succeed in completely depopulating the landscape, they at least made a thorough job of burning all human habitation. Vigdis Hafto describes how her family were the last civilians to leave Honningsvåg, as her mother had been very ill and was not fit to be moved earlier. The local doctor and priest took her and the children down to the harbour where they climbed aboard a small fishing boat. They pulled away from their hometown at dusk, just as the Germans started to raze the buildings: the fateful date was 13 November. As they moved along the fjord, the whole night sky was lit by flames and the air was full of acrid smoke. The Germans continued the despoliation of Magerøya until Christmas Eve, pillaging anything of value, burning every house and building with characteristic thoroughness and finally blowing up all the military installations which they themselves had built. Only one building was to survive in Honningsvåg – the church. Perhaps it was resistant to the flames, or possibly a soldier with a pang of conscience pulled back from his duty. Of the rest of the community, there was not a single building left.

The small boatload of evacuees made their way by night without lights to avoid attention, and it was fortunate that they were blessed by unseasonally good weather. It took many nights to thread their way the 650 kilometres to their destination at Sortland, on the Vesterålen (Western Isles). The refugee Haftos were to stay there for the next six months, until on 8 May 1945 word came that the Germans had been ordered to surrender. The dreadful ordeal was over, and even more exciting news reached them that Father was not far away, in Tromsø. Halldis, Kjersti, now aged 16, Torbjør, 12, Gunnar-Helge, 11, and Vigdis, 9, managed to find their way to Tromsø before the end of the month. Their emotional reunion was an experience shared by millions all over Europe, each one overflowing with joy, but for many also poignant with loss. The Hafto family had lost their home and all their possessions, and also Bamse, their beloved friend and companion. Many might say that the loss of a dog was insignificant in the context of their other experiences, but this was not so with the Hafto family, as subsequent events would prove.

Orlogskaptein Erling Hafto continued to serve in the Royal
Norwegian Navy, directing the task of mine clearance in northern
waters, which was vital to opening up the seaways so important
to the fabric of Norwegian life. When he was released from
service in September 1946, he was re-appointed to his pre-war job
as harbour-master at Honningsvåg, together with the additional
position of pilot-master. Ahead lay great challenges in rebuilding
the harbour business and re-establishing a home for the family.
They endured the exceptionally cold winters of 1946 and 1947
living in unheated pre-fabricated huts, and Vigdis remembers
the family's clothing being stiffly frozen by the morning!

Gradually life became more normal. A new house was built on
the ruins of the one they had lived in before the war. These were
hard years, and they often passed the time remembering happier
times before the war, and their lives with Bamse. Erling Hafto
could now tell the children about their family pet's extraordinary
adventures, of his heroism and of his sad death. But they were
not the only ones who remembered the dog, and in early 1947
a letter found its way to Honningsvåg from Dorothea St Hill
Bourne, the former secretary of the PDSA Mascot Club, who
had met Erling in London when he approached PDSA to enrol
Bamse in the Allied Forces Mascot Club in 1944. Only two
months after the date of Bamse's certificate of enrolment, Erling
had had to write again to the club, saying – 'It is with a very
heavy heart I write to tell you Bamse is dead.' Now Dorothea
had traced Erling's address and was writing to request more
information about Bamse for *They Also Serve*, her book about
animals that played an important part in uplifting the spirit
and morale of troops during the war. Her book was the first
published instance of Bamse's story, which would be told and
remembered again and again.

Bjørn Hagen, former crew member of *Thorodd* and friend of Bamse, had a very different homecoming to Erling Hafto. He finished the war as a member of the crew of KNM *Stord*, a Norwegian cruiser that was selected to escort King Haakon VII back to his people. Having heard of the terrible privations suffered by his countrymen at home, he spent much of his savings and wartime ration coupons buying useful foods and gifts for his family in Oslo – butter, eggs, flour, sugar, jam and a generous quantity of tobacco. On 7 June 1945, exactly five years to the day after the daring escape from Tromsø on HMS *Devonshire*, King Haakon sailed up Oslofjorden on the heavy cruiser HMS *Norfolk*. The flotilla included HMS *Devonshire*, completing her duty to the king after a long interval, HMS *Onslow* and KNM *Stord*. Their reception was rapturous – thousands of people were lining the quayside to welcome home their king. Bjørn remembers that sailors could kiss whomever they liked and that this was aided by the liberation of a cache of excellent German cognac!

The kissing over, it was time to make his way to the family home, where his widower father, his brothers and sisters had no reason to expect his homecoming. Unknown to him, they had been officially notified five years previously that he had died on the torpedoed battleship *Eidsvold*. His knock on the door was answered by his sister who, thinking she was seeing a ghost, started to scream hysterically whilst flinging her arms around her brother. The commotion brought the rest of the household to the door. His father was altogether more phlegmatic – 'Why, you're back! We thought you'd been sleeping on the bottom with Davy Jones!' After the shortest reflective pause he continued, 'By the way, have you brought any tobacco?'

With the general dispersal of people after a long war and with the passage of time, it is more difficult to follow what

happened to the other Norwegian sailors who were Bamse's
friends. Most of *Thorodd*'s crew returned home as soon as
possible, some remaining in the navy and most continuing at
sea. A.K. Johansen, Albert Andersen and Herman Eilertsen had
married Scottish girls and settled in Scotland. Einar Andersen,
Reidar Pedersen and Olav Nilsen took their Scottish wives back
to Norway. Olav Nilsen left the navy as a lieutenant commander
and returned to his pre-war job as a coastal pilot until he retired.
Many years after the war, he was instructed to pilot his old
wartime command, *Syrian*, into port. By the most remarkable
of afterthoughts, he remembered that he still had the wartime
key to his cabin. When he inserted it into the cabin lock he was
delighted to find that it still fitted perfectly.

Olav's son, Dr Willie Nilsen, describes how the legend of
Bamse was passed on to the next generation. 'I believe that
stories about Bamse have been told to many of the children of
the crew of *Thorodd*, and the other naval vessels stationed in
Dundee. As all parents know, it isn't possible to change such
stories around, as children will immediately object. The stories
will live on, therefore, in their original form, and will be as close
to the truth as possible. Bamse deserves to be remembered as a
positive recollection about the war, and as a symbol of the good
relationship between Scotland and Norway.'

Willie later undertook his medical degree at Dundee University.
In his final year of studies in 1974, Olav came to Dundee, and
he and Willie revisited the docks and other places associated
with the war, particularly the quayside where Bamse had saved
his life, and Lunan Bay where he had nearly been bombed
into oblivion. Even in the 1970s, Willie was made aware of the
close wartime relationship between the local people and the
Norwegians. 'During my days at university I could be at a pub

when I got a pint I had not ordered,' he recalls. 'The publican would then point to an older person who would say, by way of explanation, that he had been friendly with the Norwegians during the war.'

In the summer of 1949, 10 years after they had last seen their family pet, Vigdis, then aged 14, and Gunnar-Helge, 16, set out on a remarkable pilgrimage in devoted memory of Bamse. By this time Honningsvåg was busy once more with shipping, particularly deep-sea trawlers, many of which were from Britain. Amongst the trawler captains was a friend from the war, George Noble from Grimsby, who was one of the many visitors to the family home. When Erling told him the story of Bamse and of his burial at Montrose, George suggested a summer trip for the two youngest children to visit the grave. This was greeted with enthusiasm and probably some apprehension for it would be an adventurous trip of several thousands of kilometres by sea and land. It would certainly expand the teenagers' horizons and help with their English language studies. At a time of continuing shortages of basic commodities, Halldis somehow managed to obtain a small piece of tartan cloth and made a new dress for Vigdis and a tie for Gunnar-Helge. They posed together for a formal photograph modelling their unusual Scottish attire.

As there was not enough room on board one trawler for both to travel together, Vigdis left home first, with George Noble, on 15 July 1949, three days before her brother, who followed in another boat. It was midsummer, and it was snowing! Brother and sister were re-united at Grimsby, where they stayed with the Noble family. George Noble himself accompanied the two children up to Scotland and they arrived in Montrose to visit the grave on 2 August 1949. The visit attracted the attention of the press, and feature articles appeared in the *Dundee Courier* and the *Montrose Standard*, both pieces quoting extensively from Dorothea St Hill Bourne's book *They Also Serve*. The visitors were pleased to find that the grave was very neat and tidy and had been edged with granite setts, or cobblestones. Anne Ross had faithfully maintained the site and had arranged for a new cross to be made by Arbuthnott the boat builders with an additional plaque attached below the cross spar. Anne herself made a fresh inscription in the wood, using a hot poker. Her wording has been kept until the present day.

ST BERNARD
"BAMSE"
FAITHFUL FRIEND
OF ALL ON BOARD
THE THORODD
LARGEST DOG OF
THE ALLIED NAVAL FORCES

Anne promised the two children that she would continue to look after the grave as long as she was able, and she kept this promise for the next 20 years. It was an epic journey for two teenagers in those post-war days, and, for Vigdis in particular, it fixed in her a determination to preserve the memory of Bamse. That determination has brought her back to the same spot in the sand dunes of Montrose on four further occasions over the past 55 years.

The 1950s were a time of great reconstruction and development in Britain, as in the rest of Europe. There was wholesale clearance of war-damaged and substandard buildings, and extensive new building programmes throughout the country. New industries were being created and factories were springing up. Montrose was badly in need of substantial investment, having been through a period of recession before the war. It was therefore very good news when the pharmaceutical company Glaxo Laboratories Ltd decided to build a new factory in the town to exploit the recent discovery of active steroids. They were looking to develop a piece of land in the sand dunes at the river mouth – which included the site of Bamse's grave!

If the Montrose harbour-master, Mr H. McLennan, had not had the courtesy to contact his counterpart in Honningsvåg, it is most likely that the bulldozers would have erased Bamse's memory forever. In 1952 he wrote to Erling Hafto, explaining that the proposed new factory would be erected on ground containing Bamse's remains and asking if the Hafto family would have any objection to the grave being removed. Not surprisingly, the Hafto family asked that Bamse's remains be respected and, out of consideration for their feelings, the Montrose harbour-master ensured that the grave was saved. Although it would lie on its land, Glaxo Laboratories agreed to divert the perimeter fence to allow the grave to remain accessible to the public. That is why, to this day, the fence has an accommodating detour in it. It is also why, when Anne Ross finally gave up tending to the grave in the late 1960s, Glaxo took over the continuing responsibility for the upkeep of the grave site.

It says much about the memories of Bamse that Anne Ross in particular, and others as well, maintained his grave over the decades when most people were looking forward, and not backwards to the recollections of an unpleasant war. There are reports of visits to the grave by travellers from Norway, veterans of the war and their relatives. A regular visitor was Bamse's old shipmate Fritz Egge, who came on many occasions until his death in 2000. He so impressed his friend Captain Johan Campbell Andersen with his devotion to the memory of the dog that later on Johan and his wife Liv began to visit Montrose themselves and became central to the Bamse revival in Norway.

'Vikings land in Montrose', announced the *Montrose Standard* in July 1964, reporting the arrival of three torpedo boats of 22 MTB Squadron Royal Norwegian Navy, the *Erle*, the *Gribb* and the *Tjeld*, on the 23rd of that month. The Royal Norwegian Navy had not forgotten its mascot Bamse, and Kontreadmiral Voltersvik ordered this courtesy visit to coincide with the twentieth anniversary of his death. Lieutenant Commander Robert Saether, who was one of the executive officers in 1964, wrote very much later, in 2004, that they had found that the grave was well kept, but were surprised to see that the cross had been mistakenly painted in Icelandic colours, and they had quickly repainted it in the correct ones! There was a small graveside ceremony attended by the ships' crews and local army cadets, at which they laid a wreath of flowers. The press, however, seemed to think that a football match between the Norwegians and a Montrose select team was more newsworthy.

Three months later, in October, 22 MTB Squadron paid a visit to Honningsvåg, where Commander Erling Hafto was still harbour-master. Executive Officer Saether proudly told him that they had visited Bamse's grave, that they had redecorated the cross and had placed flowers there. Erling said that he already knew because he had been presented with the invoice for the flowers by the navy West Coast Command!

It was, in fact, to be another 20 years, 1984, before there was a real resurgence in the story of the great St Bernard, although in 1983 the bestselling British author Jilly Cooper featured Bamse, with an illustration, in her popular book *Animals in War*.

'Montrose police are making enquiries into the death of a dog 40 years ago', was the cryptic headline in the *Dundee Evening Telegraph* on 7 March 1984. That story heralded a renewed interest in Bamse in Norway and in Scotland, and it certainly caught the attention of the readership. An Oslo writer called Otto Opstad was researching for a book about war dogs and also hoped to make a television film about Bamse. Otto had written to the police station in Montrose asking if they knew the location of the grave of the famous Norwegian dog. The police were baffled by this enquiry, but fortunately they had the idea of referring the question to the *Dundee Evening Telegraph*. The answer was quickly forthcoming, with around a hundred people contacting the paper in Dundee and 40 getting in touch with the police in Montrose. A Montrose resident wrote, 'You Norwegians should know that we Scots will not forget our Allied friends from the last war – whether they have two legs – or four!'

Newspaper articles now began to appear on both sides of the North Sea, and Bamse once again began to capture public imagination. The Norwegian Navy was alerted to the approach of the 40th anniversary of the dog's death, and this time planned to send a significant delegation to Montrose. Two submarines, *Utsira* and *Utvaer*, visited Montrose from 3 to 4 July 1984, bringing with them the senior officer commanding Norwegian submarines, Captain R. Skarlo. The visit brought out people in their hundreds, and a large graveside ceremony was attended by local dignitaries. Guests of honour were Vigdis Hafto and her daughter Kirsten. In recognition of her devoted care of the grave, Captain Skarlo presented Anne Ross with a Royal Norwegian

Navy commemorative plaque. Widely reported, this event put Bamse's story back in the news.

The television film about Bamse was broadcast in 1984, at the time of Norwegian Constitution Day, 17 May. The interest in this and the publicity surrounding Otto Opstad's researches had a further unexpected outcome. The Norwegian animal protection association Dyrebeskyttelsen (the equivalent of the British RSPCA) picked up on the story. Particularly captivated was Gerd Darner, the vice president of the association, and a well-known poet and wildlife artist. Championed by Gerd, Dyrebeskyttelsen created a new animal order of recognition, Norges Hundeorden (Norway's Dog Order) with Bamse as the very first recipient! On 30 September 1984, amid a blaze of publicity, a handsome bronze plaque was handed over to Vigdis Hafto. It bore the inscription (translated):

ANIMAL PROTECTION HONOUR PRIZE
NORWAY'S DOG ORDER
IS AWARDED TO
WAR DOG 'BAMSE'
WITH GRATITUDE FOR
EFFORTS
FIDELITY
INTELLIGENCE

An accompanying citation added 'for war service 9th February 1940 until 22nd July 1944'. The plaque and citation are now displayed with other Bamse memorabilia in the Norwegian Marinemuseet (Maritime Museum) at Horten near Oslo. All of this renewed interest was consolidated in the book that Otto Opstad subsequently published in 1987, *Skipshunden Bamse og andre Brukshunder* (*Ship's Dog Bamse and other War Dogs*).

The resurgence of interest in the great St Bernard dog seems to have settled into a pattern of 10-year cycles, for it was another decade before Bamse's story surfaced again. In 1994 a new book, *Silent Heroes* by Evelyn le Chêne, was published, with a photograph of Bamse on the front cover and a whole chapter devoted to his life. The book has been so popular that it has remained in print ever since, with a new edition published in 2008. This again attracted the interest of the press, which ran several follow-up articles. The year was also the 50th anniversary of Bamse's death and the Norwegian Navy did not forget, sending the submarine KNM *Kunna*, under the command of Lieutenant Commander Erik Boe with a crew of 25 men, on a visit to Montrose, although this time it was a quieter affair than in 1984.

After another decade, the story and the memory of Bamse again resurfaced on a scale not seen before, and with a more permanent outcome.

11

The Lady in the Hat

The year 2004 marked the 60th anniversary of Operation Overlord, the D-Day landings in the final phase of World War II. The young sailors, soldiers and airmen who had risked all at that time were entering their eighties. There was a feeling that their wartime sacrifices should not be allowed to be forgotten, and there was a huge resurgence of interest in the war and its veterans. Scarcely a day went by without a newspaper article or television feature poignantly observing the contributions of the older generation, and there was wide media coverage of the D-Day veterans who converged in pilgrimage on the Normandy beaches.

It was at this time that the Norwegian Navy again decided to commemorate Bamse's death, and planned to send the crew of the submarine *Utvaer* to Montrose. The news was received by the town's harbour-master, Captain Harry Johansen, son of A.K. Johansen, who had been a *Thorodd* crew member and great companion of Bamse. Captain Johansen brought the announcement to the attention of the members of the board of the Montrose Port Authority, one of whom was a small lady who always wore a trademark large Stetson-style hat, even at board meetings. She was Henny King, who had been appointed to the board to raise the port authority's public profile, which she was very well equipped to do, having led a full and colourful life working in journalism, education, the arts, media and public relations. Her greatest challenge and achievement previously had been as director, over two years, of the hugely successful City of Dundee octocentenary (800th anniversary) celebrations. She undertook this with such vigour and verve that she became a well-known celebrity in the east of Scotland, where she is universally known as 'Henny – the lady in the hat'.

Henny was immediately captivated by the story of the Norwegian dog, and decided that the Norwegian Navy visit should be celebrated in style. With the resources of the port authority and the backing of GlaxoSmithKline (formerly Glaxo Laboratories Ltd), but with only a few weeks until the event, Henny threw herself into her latest challenge in a frenzy of activity. Her remarkable media contacts resulted in many column inches of advanced cover, with special pullout supplements included. On the day, a crowd of hundreds, which included local dignitaries, representatives of the Royal Navy, a sea cadet band, a piper, and Harriet the St Bernard representing Bamse assembled near the grave to welcome Lieutenant Commander Øistein Jensen and the crew of *Utvaer*. Henny even found a World War II vintage double-decker bus as transport for the VIPs! There followed a very moving service of remembrance led by local minister Reverend Graeme Bruce at which Vigdis Hafto spoke emotionally about the significance of Bamse to her family and to the crew of *Thorodd*. She said, 'For me and my family, Bamse was a part of our hopes and prayers for peace and safe return to Norway for both the dog, and our father. I guess it is fair to say that we shared these hopes with the crew of *Thorodd*.' Lieutenant Commander Jensen spoke of the special wartime relationship between Norway and Scotland, as symbolised by Bamse, saying 'These people left home to fight a war far away from home, putting a lot of anxiety and fear amongst the sailors that were here. And now the sailors from Norway had a second home in Scotland. For sailors here in Montrose and especially those on the minesweeper *Thorodd* there was a special friend that brought a sense of home and family to the sailors and officers – and that was the ship's dog Bamse. Bamse had a special place in the hearts of people, in Montrose and in the Norwegian Navy. The memory of Bamse stands today as a symbol of cohesion, comradeship and care: values as important today as then.'

At the end of the service, the small lady with the hat stepped forward to sum up. After the usual formalities, Henny added, 'This is a truly fantastic story, really much better than Greyfriars Bobby in Edinburgh. It must be kept going – it should be known around the world. Maybe the people of Montrose should think of some sort of permanent memorial to Bamse, so that the story will live on . . .' As she stepped back, the press photographers moved forward to capture an image of the St Bernard and the assembled crew. Scarcely a newspaper in Britain or in Norway did not carry a picture of Harriet the St Bernard in a Norwegian sailor's hat, posing by the grave with the Norwegian sailors. Bamse's story was news, big news, once again.

In the crowd, there more out of curiosity than from any great knowledge of the story, was a local family doctor, Andrew Orr. As he left the scene, Henny's words repeated themselves in his mind over and over again, and he thought about what would be a fitting memorial to Bamse. Montrose was already acknowledged as having the best collection of statues and sculptures of any town of comparable size in Scotland. It was also the home of William Lamb, arguably one of the greatest Scottish sculptors of the 20th century. A statue it would have to be! Andrew was a founding director of the Montrose Heritage Trust, a charitable body whose aims include promoting the royal burgh through its historical and cultural assets. It seemed that a new and significant statue of the legendary Norwegian sea dog, and the resurrection of his story would serve this purpose rather well. The trustees, under their chairman Dr Tony Sutton, agreed, and in due course the Montrose Bamse Project was officially launched. Andrew was appointed to be the project chairman, and Henny was recruited to assist and advise as project director.

News of the appeal to raise £50,000 for a statue was picked up eagerly by the newspapers. This was only the start of extraordinary interest and future support from the media. Henny, a public relations professional, and Andrew, a family doctor, were an unusual but very effective partnership, and they threw themselves into raising such a sum. Their work ranged from the simplest of tasks, such as writing letters, through to organising major events. Anyone who has been involved in fundraising in a small town will know that it can be a daunting task, but there was such great interest in Bamse's story and so much publicity during the campaign that there was never any real doubt about its eventual success. Early major donations from GlaxoSmithKline in Britain and the charitable Kavli Foundation in Bergen were followed by others from the Royal Norwegian Navy and the Norwegian Seamans' Union. The bulk of the funds, however, came from hundreds and hundreds of individual donations, not only from Scotland and Norway, but also from all corners of the world. Captain Johan Campbell Andersen became Bamse's ambassador and fundraising co-ordinator in Norway, whilst John Stevenson, husband of Jean Stevenson the Montrose Heritage Trust treasurer, kept everything shipshape at Montrose. In this way, the campaign was sustained by the generosity and support of countless people and organisations.

With funds starting to come in, Tony Sutton assembled a small group to draw up specifications and select a sculptor for the statue. The group included the local but internationally recognised artist Dr James Morrison, award-winning architect Ben Tindall, sculptor Dr Alistair Ross and Norman Atkinson, director of cultural services for Angus Council. Such was the interest in the project that unsolicited as well as invited applications came in from all over Britain. The renowned Scottish sculptor Alan Herriot, who has a particular affinity with military and animal sculptures, was chosen from tough competition. Alan quickly threw himself into researching his subject, and was particularly amused and pleased when Norwegian veteran Reidar Pedersen viewed an early model of the statue and berated him for getting the scale of the chest and forelegs wrong. Much later, when viewing the finished version, Reidar declared that Alan's statue was 'exactly as I remember him – he has got it just right'.

It was around this time that the erroneous claims that Bamse had been awarded the PDSA Dickin Medal came to light. It was quickly established that he had not received the award, which was scarcely surprising as it had only been instituted a year before he died and he was a Norwegian rather than a British dog. Andrew Orr discovered, however, that PDSA had made a number of retrospective awards of the PDSA Dickin Medal. It had also instituted another award, the PDSA Gold Medal, the equivalent of the George Cross, which was awarded to animals for saving lives whilst not actually under enemy fire. He wondered if Bamse, as a member of the Allied Forces, might not, even after all the intervening years, be considered for one of these awards for his heroic actions.

Andrew was gathering a great deal of information already known and published about Bamse's life. At an early stage, a well-respected newspaper reporter had asked him, grinning, 'Surely you don't really believe all those stories about the dog, do you? They're just apocryphal!'

Now, however, there were people coming forward who had actually known Bamse, and who were able to confirm accurately many of the anecdotes that were already part of his tradition. New accounts and stories continued to emerge. Andrew's work as a family doctor brought him in touch with patients who had private memories that had lain dormant for more than 60 years. All the newspaper coverage encouraged others to make contact, while some Scottish and Norwegian veterans and their families had to be tracked down by detective work. Andrew quickly realised that, far from being apocryphal, the stories about Bamse were not only true, but also extraordinary, quite beyond the normal expectations of canine behaviour.

Soon enough, evidence had been gathered to make a formal citation to PDSA Council for a gallantry award, and this was submitted in March 2006. Central to the citation were three signed and witnessed statements. The first was by Vigdis Hafto, verifying what her father had said about Bamse's inspirational courage when he was in enemy action. The second was by Dr Willie Nilsen, who confirmed how Bamse had saved his father's life during the knife attack at Dundee harbour. Reidar Pedersen, the surviving veteran, gave the third statement, describing how Bamse had saved the life of the sailor who had fallen overboard from *Thorodd* into the fast-moving waters of the River Tay.

In May, the news came, with a fanfare of press coverage, that Bamse had been awarded the PDSA Gold Medal for gallantry. This is the only time that PDSA has awarded its Gold Medal retrospectively for deeds performed so many years before. The presentation ceremony took place at the National Trust for Scotland's historic House of Dun near Montrose on 22 July 2006, 62 years to the day after the heroic St Bernard had died. In an emotional moment, Mr Freddie Bircher, PDSA chairman, placed the magnificent medal into the hand of Vigdis Hafto whose life, from her childhood onwards, had been so affected by that of her family pet, Bamse.

The sight of tall sailing ships is a familiar one to so many people who have witnessed them gathering for the Tall Ships races at major ports across Europe. Not for many decades, however, had the Royal Burgh of Montrose seen anything like the Norwegian *Statsraad Lehmkhul*, the world's largest sailing barque, as she elegantly glided into Montrose port at the beginning of July 2005. At a length of 84 metres, and with a 48-metre main mast, she dwarfed the buildings on the harbour front. Hundreds of people flocked to see the magnificent sight, and they must have been surprised to see *Lehmkhul* flying a large nautical banner from her yardarms, on which was a giant picture of Bamse's logo, together with a couplet:

REMEMBER BAMSE, HEROIC AND CLEVER,
SCOTLAND AND NORWAY ARE FRIENDS FOREVER!

The Lehmkhul Foundation, which operates the ship, had agreed that this visit could be used to promote the Montrose Bamse Project's appeal for funds for Bamse's statue, and it proved to be very effective indeed. News coverage with pictures of the beautiful ship drew several thousands of visitors to an open day on board, with a pipe band, Highland dancers and other entertainments on the quay alongside. The crew, trainees and passengers of Lehmkhul enjoyed their visit to Montrose so much that she was back in port in August 2006, again helping to contribute to the statue funds.

The Lehmkhul visits were the most spectacular amongst a series of events staged by Henny and Andrew during the campaign. Other events included a visit with a St Bernard, Murphy, to the Scottish Parliament, where a motion was presented and accepted, endorsing the Bamse Project. A grand reception was held at Dundee on board historic HMS *Unicorn*, wartime headquarter ship of the Norwegian minesweeper division. There was a children's art competition and exhibition entitled 'The Adventures of Bamse', which produced some very impressive work indeed, showing that yet another generation had been captivated by Bamse's story. The 12 prize-winning works were so good that it was decided to publish them as a series of postcards, so that Bamse's tale could spread even further.

In July 2006, Jilly Cooper opened a major exhibition celebrating the rôle of animals in wartime, 'The Animals' War', at the Imperial War Museum in London. Bamse featured in the exhibition in the form of a smaller version or maquette, in bronze, of the sculpture being made by Alan Herriot. This was seen and stroked by tens of thousands of visitors over the next 10 months, and was subsequently purchased by the Marinemuseet at Horten, where it is now on display.

Henny, the lady in the hat, has a remarkable talent for finding an angle or an image that will appeal to the media, and, of course, a dog with a story like Bamse's is irresistible. Through her efforts, Andrew and Henny compiled a scrapbook of nearly 200 newspaper cuttings about the project, including articles from local, national and Norwegian newspapers. There were radio interviews from Dundee and Montrose to Alberta in Canada, short advance features on Scottish TV news, and national live news broadcasts when the unveiling of the statue at last took place.

Even though Bamse's tale does not end, the story of the statue had to come to a conclusion. Alan Herriot's long and passionate labour had culminated in a massive bronze, one and a half times life-size, being cast at the Powderhall Foundry in Edinburgh by (the aptly named) Brian Caster. An excellent site on Montrose's ancient waterfront had been identified and made available by the port authority, following which Angus Council developed it as a new open space adjacent to the splendid bridge across the river, which was opened in 2005. In a delicate operation, a crane lifted a four-tonne block of granite into position, followed by the installation of the statue, which quickly disappeared from public view beneath covers. So much effort by so many people and organisations was finally drawing to a close, and a date and time had been fixed to unveil the latest addition to Montrose's collection of fine statuary.

At seven o' clock on the morning of 17 October 2006, Andrew Orr stood on the quayside of Montrose and mentally checked off the arrangements for the great unveiling day. The police had closed off Wharf Street and diverted the traffic; some workmen were erecting crowd-control barriers, while others cleaned the street and put the finishing touches to flowerbeds. A large marquee had been erected. It was the culmination of months of detailed planning, for the day had taken on a special significance from the moment Prince Andrew, HRH The Duke of York, had agreed to unveil the statue. A distinguished naval veteran of the Falklands War, the prince was well suited to understanding the Scottish–Norwegian naval relationship of World War II. GlaxoSmithKline had continued its generous support of the Bamse story and project, and as ever had contributed substantially to the arrangements for the ceremony, after which the prince was to visit the pharmaceutical company's factory.

At about eight o'clock a pretty girl had taken up a lonely position at the barrier opposite the statue. 'You're here early,' Andrew Orr commented.

'I came up on the first train from Edinburgh!' she explained, and told him that her name was Carla and she was far from her native Argentina. 'I really wanted to be in a good position to see Bamse. I have loved his story ever since I first heard of it. And of course, I might get to meet Prince Andrew!'

Four hours later, Wharf Street was transformed. Several thousand members of the public had gathered behind the barriers, many of them children from all of the local schools. Lathallan Preparatory School pipe band was parading in front of the crowd, with a large St Bernard called Brit in the vanguard. The marquee was filling with dignitaries and visitors, including many who had come from Norway. Representatives of the Royal Norwegian Navy and the Royal Navy were lined up behind the shrouded statue. Ranks of media reporters, photographers and cameramen were being held back by the police. Everything was as it should be. And then it was all happening – the arrival of His Royal Highness, the introductions, the speeches and the moment when the covering of the statue was loosened and pulled away. It seemed that there was a total silence – it probably lasted a few milliseconds – and then there was a universal roar of approval. This was it for Andrew, Henny and the Montrose Heritage Trust: the end point of so much effort and preparation, and the public approved.

Prince Andrew ran well over his schedule in meeting and talking to the marquee guests and the waiting crowds. He was particularly surprised and delighted to be introduced to Vigdis Hafto and to make the connection between her childhood family pet and the war dog he had just commemorated. The prince remarked, 'I don't quite understand – why was it that Bamse actually went to the war?'

'Oh that's simple!' said Vigdis, 'My mother said to my father, "You can't expect me to continue to look after the children and him on my own. There won't be enough to eat!"'

Captain Johan Campbell Andersen was able to tell him about the fundraising success in Norway and of the great interest about Bamse in his country. The prince was energetic in meeting and talking to people, especially the children, in the larger crowds outside. Andrew Orr spotted Carla, squashed against the barrier, and, guiding the prince across, introduced her. Her lovely smile showed that wishes do, for those who get up early, come true.

It would be fair to say that few speeches on these sorts of official occasions are memorable, and that many are best forgotten! However, this was not the case on this occasion. The main television news channels that evening carried long excerpts from Prince Andrew's speech, while the newspapers quoted extensively from his speech, as well as that of the Norwegian consul in Scotland, Bjørn Eilertsen, who brought a message of greeting from King Harald V of Norway. Bjørn emphasised the importance of the ties between his country and Scotland:

> It is when times get tough that we really get to know our friends, and this applies to nations as well as individuals. In Great Britain, Norwegian sailors and soldiers found hospitality, friendship and hope during dark years. Many Norwegians ended up in Scotland. Many, including a dog, arrived in Montrose. And this dog was

Bamse who was to become a symbol of bravery, devotion and also freedom. And Bamse is also the reason why we are here today, and it is really a fitting tribute that the Bamse statue will preserve his memory and cement the special relationship between the Norwegian and the Scottish people.

In his unscripted but well-judged speech, Prince Andrew caught the mood of the moment:

Animals, and particularly dogs, have a special place in many people's hearts, and they have been a part of military service for a great many years. Bamse, this particular dog, served at a peculiar time in history and was an incredible dog in what he actually stood for, and what he did and why he did it. Many of us will find it difficult to understand how a dog can have that sort of loyalty, not only to his own shipmates, but also to the people of Montrose. What was going on in that dog's head we will never know, but the people of the Norwegian Navy, the people of the Royal Navy and the people of Montrose hold this dog in the highest esteem, and I think that it is only right and proper that a statue should be here to remember the loyalty and friendship that this dog showed in the dark days of the war, and also to remind us what loyalty actually means.

Postscript
Bamse returns to Honningsvåg

Almost 70 years after he left Honningsvåg Bamse returned home – in a manner of speaking. His inspirational story, the success of the Montrose Bamse Project and the wonderful statue erected at Montrose Harbour were all keenly observed in Norway. As a boy Sigurd Berg-Hansen had known both Erling Hafto and Oscar Jensen in Honningsvåg, and he had learned from them about the war, about *Thorodd* and about Bamse. He felt that Bamse should be commemorated in his home town, as in Scotland. Bamse's story would help to remind people what had happened in Mageroya during the war; it would commemorate the sacrifice of those who left, never to return, and it would pass the lessons learned on to the next generation. With the backing of Mayor Kristina Hansen, the Kommune and Port of North Cape, Sigurd launched their *Bamseprosjekt* to raise funds for their own full-sized bronze statue of the famous dog. In only eleven months they had achieved their objective and commissioned a replica of the one at Montrose, which will be seen by a quarter of a million visitors who pass through Honningsvåg every year.

So it was that, on 19 June 2009, a parade assembled at Honningsvåg's War Memorial, in front of the church, the only building to survive the war and the heart of a thriving modern town. The combined bands of the Skolekorps (Honningsvåg school brass band) and Lathallan School pipe band, specially flown over for the occasion, filled the air with music. After a short wreath-laying ceremony the bands led the parade down the town's main street, drawing in almost the whole population behind it. Reaching the quayside everyone assembled around the shrouded statue of Bamse. Amongst those who had travelled from Scotland were the Provost of Angus, Ruth Leslie-Melville, Tony Sutton with members of the Montrose Heritage Trust, and the sculptor Alan Herriot. Vigdis Hafto, Willie Nilsen, and Christine Jensen formed direct links with the story of *Thorodd* and her ship's dog. Dignitaries and supporters from Norway, Sweden and even Canada swelled the crowd.

In a moving gesture, two children from each school performed the unveiling of the statue, which was greeted with enthusiastic applause. In her speech, Mayor Kristina Hansen welcomed Bamse back to his original home, emphasising that his presence and his story will sustain the memory of the dark war years, whilst drawing Norway and Scotland closer together. 'If you look at a map you will see that our Bamse is looking south-west towards Montrose, and your Bamse is facing north-east towards Honningsvåg. This will keep us in mind of each other in years to come.'

Angus Whitson
Andrew Orr
July 2009

Sources

Books

St Hill Bourne, Dorothea, *They Also Serve* (Winchester
    Publications, London: 1947)
Cooper, Jilly, *Animals in War* (Heinemann, London: 1983,
    2000)
Opstad, Otto, *Skipshunden Bamse* (Nye Atheneum, Oslo:
    1987)
Le Chêne, Evelyn, *Silent Heroes* (Souvenir, London: 1994,
    2008)
Petterøe, Anders, *Fem År På Banjeren* (Delfinen Forlag,
    Frederikstad: 1995)
Abelsen, Frank, *Norske Mineveipere* (Marinemuseet, Horten:
    1999)
Hansen, Eric R., *From War to Peace* (Nordkapplitterature,
    Honningsvåg: 2003)

Newspapers

Montrose Review
Montrose Standard
Dundee Courier
People's Journal
Dundee Evening Telegraph

Selected Websites

www.warsailors.com
www.pdsa.org.uk
www.frigateunicorn.org
www.naval-history.net
www.pigtrail.uark.edu/people/rcordell/defense/minewar.html
uboat.net/allies/merchants/ship.html?shipID=3467
www.bamsemontrose.co.uk

Acknowledgements

The authors are indebted to the following organisations and people who have provided general and sometimes specific information, advice and help, and/or have given permission to print extracts and images. Apologies are offered to anyone who may have been inadvertently missed out.

Organisations

Alpha Images (Ronnie Carmichael); Birlinn Ltd (Hugh Andrew, Andrew Simmons, Sarah Ream); Central Library, Dundee; GlaxoSmithKline plc (Susan Jessop); Imperial War Museum London (Terry Charman); Marinemuseet, Horten (Commander Hans Petter Oset); Montrose Heritage Trust (Tony Sutton, Jean Stevenson, Dugal Beedie, Alan Doe, Kitty Ritchie, Jonathan Stansfeld, Sandy Munro); Montrose Library; Printshop, Montrose (Derek Addison, Grant McMaster); Riksarkivet, Oslo (Lief Thingsrud); Royal Archives of Norway (Lise Harlem); office of HRH The Duke of York; images and other information from Nordkappmuseet, Honningsvåg (Kjersti Skavhaug); chapter 5 extract from the *People's Journal* courtesy and © D.C. Thomson & Co., Ltd; chapter 9 extract courtesy of Souvenir Press Ltd;

gold-medal picture and other information from PDSA (Isabel George, Claire Evans).

Individuals

Vigdis Hafto and children (Steinar and Kirsten); Willie Nilsen; Harry and Eileen Johansen; Johan Campbell Andersen; Hilary Foxworthy; John Aitken; Anna Palfreman; Forbes Inglis; Bjørn Eilertsen; Henny King; Pam and Murray Coutts; William and Violet Coull; Richard Neville; Colin Silver; Michelle Goring (Bamse logo design); Jilly Cooper; Elizabeth Whitson; Antonia Orr; Victoria Willis (authors' photography).

Individual Testimonial Sources

The authors are particularly grateful to the many individuals who have contributed their memories to this book. Some material has come from filmed interviews (supplied by the Marinemuseet, Horten), and some from personal interviews carried out between 2005 and 2008. The individuals are listed in the order that they are introduced as dramatis personae in the text, followed by the names of those who have related the story in brackets (where this is applicable). We apologise if this process has slipped, or if there are any unintentional omissions.

Erling Hafto and family (Vigdis Hafto); Alf N. Thomassen; Olav August Johan Nilsen (Willie Nilsen); Norman Lawrance; Bjørn Hagen; Herman Eilertsen and Dorothy Brown; Clement Meyer (Nan Meyer); Anders Petterøe; Anders Kristian Larsen; Albert Andersen; Einar Andersen and Rena Grilli (Louise Hood

neé Grilli); Henry 'A.K.' Johansen (Harry Johansen); Henry
Berthling and Ruby Low (Peter Low); Reidar Pedersen; Oscar
Jensen and Margaret Crichton (Heather Cochrane); Jacob
Berg and Elizabeth Younger (Elizabeth Berg neé Younger);
Fritz Egge (Johan Campell Andersen); Bob Milne; William W.
Coull; Andrew 'Codling' Mearns (Andrew Mearns, junior);
Alex Henderson; Doug Anderson; Donald Cooper; Jack Harper;
Jessie Moig (now Paton); Tom Frost; Anne Ross (Moira Ross);
Jean Wallace (now Butler-Madden); Lilian Winchester (Knut
Nicolaysen); Helen Dempster (now Whitfield); John McPherson
(John McPherson, grandson); Anne Urquhart; Margaret
McDermid; Willie Rice (Dennis Rice); Robert Whyte; James
MacDonald; Ronald C Webster; Duncan Strang; David Oswald;
Robert Saether.

Index

Note: The Norwegian characters 'å' and 'ø' are sorted as if they were the English letters 'a' and 'o'. 'Passim' indicates scattered references over a page range